PRAYER
STILL WORKS

Kenneth E. Sullivan, Jr.

Printed by: Prize Publishing House, LLC in the United States of America.

First printing edition 2021.
Prize Publishing House
P.O. Box 9856, Chesapeake, VA 23321
www.PrizePublishingHouse.com

Library of Congress Control Number: 2021922956

ISBN (Paperback): 978-1-7379751-1-3
ISBN (E-Book): 978-1-7379751-2-0

CONTENTS

DEDICATION 1

INTRODUCTION 3

SECTION 1: GIVE IT TO GOD 5

    CHAPTER 1: HANNAH REQUESTS TO GIVE BIRTH 11

    CHAPTER 2: HANNAH RELEASES HER BURDEN 17

    CHAPTER 3: HANNAH RECEIVES HER BLESSING 23

SECTION 2: PUSH (PRAY UNTIL SOMETHING
HAPPENS) 27

    CHAPTER 4: HEZEKIAH'S DISTRESS 32

    CHAPTER 5: HEZEKIAH'S DECISION 39

    CHAPTER 6: HEZEKIAH'S DELIVERY 44

SECTION 3: GOD WILL TURN IT AROUND 49

    CHAPTER 7: THE REPORT FOR HEZEKIAH 53

    CHAPTER 8: THE RESOLVE OF HEZEKIAH 60

    CHAPTER 9: THE REVERSAL FOR HEZEKIAH 67

SECTION 4: GET READY FOR RAIN 71

    CHAPTER 10: ELIJAH PERCEIVED THAT IT WOULD RAIN 75

CHAPTER 11: ELIJAH PRAYED THAT IT WOULD RAIN 81

CHAPTER 12: ELIJAH PREPARED FOR THE RAIN 88

SECTION 5: PRAYER IS STILL THE ANSWER.................91

CHAPTER 13: EXHORTATION TO PRAY 94

CHAPTER 14: THE EFFECTIVENESS OF PRAYER 100

CHAPTER 15: THE EXAMPLE OF PRAYER...........................107

SECTION 6: GOD IS WAITING ON YOUR CALL 111

CHAPTER 16: A PERSONAL REQUEST 114

CHAPTER 17: A PROMISE TO RESPOND 120

CHAPTER 18: A PROFOUND REWARD 126

SECTION 7: GETTING ALONE WITH GOD...................131

CHAPTER 19: PRAYER…DONE ON SCHEDULE....................135

CHAPTER 20: PRAYER…DONE IN SOLITUDE 143

CHAPTER 21: PRAYER…DONE TO GAIN STRENGTH 148

CONCLUSION...152

REFERENCES..157

DEDICATION

This book is dedicated to several special people whose prayer lives have been a blessing to me for many, many years.

First, to the members of New Direction Church in Indianapolis, Indiana, it is only by your effective, fervent prayers that we have been leading people to better lives for 15 years. May God continue to bless you, grow you, and use you to build His kingdom by the power of your prayer life.

Second, to my father, Dr. Kenneth E. Sullivan, Sr., the man who taught me to discipline myself and spend time with God on a daily basis. Dad, I am forever grateful for your example of what a praying man looks like. Without your exhortation to prioritize my prayer life, I would not have what I have, see what I see, nor know what I know. Thank you.

Third, to the Extended Hands Prayer Ministry at New Direction Church, the women and men who labor and spend so much time covering me, my family, and our entire congregation in prayer mean so much to me. God has indeed blessed me by the word of your effectual, fervent intercession.

Finally, to my wife Roxie, a quiet storm whose daily prayers for me have made me the man, the husband, the father, the son, the brother, the pastor, and the leader I am today. I thank God always for the gift you are in my life.

INTRODUCTION

One of my team members asked me why, of all of the subjects I espouse regularly, did I choose to write a book about prayer. The answer was simple: if we ever needed prayer before, we need it right now.

Prayer is one of the most important disciplines every disciple needs to develop. It is also something every single person can do, anytime and anywhere. Even if you don't have a Bible, you still have a voice, a mind, and a way to speak to and hear from God.

Jesus gave His disciples three major disciplines: fasting, giving, and prayer. He instructed us to pray in private to position ourselves to receive blessings in public. God wants us to get before Him to speak to Him, and He wants us to get before Him and hear from Him. Prayer is not a monologue; it is dialogue. It is a chance for us to hear from Heaven, have an audience with God, and receive instruction, direction, and comfort from our Source.

With technological advances, information at our fingertips, and access to neighbors from across the world, we have become more dependent on what our eyes see, our ears hear, and our minds conceive. Based on a recent Pew Study, the number of people who describe themselves as Christian has decreased over the past ten years, from 77% to 65%, while the "religiously unaffiliated" has increased from 17% to 26%(www.pewforum.org). As fewer people are professing faith in God, disease runs rampant across the world; international affairs continue in a state of unrest; addiction, poverty, violence, and social injustice continue to decimate our communities; people are making choices out of hopelessness and despair, and the voice of the church grows softer and softer. If we ever needed a reminder about how to plug into power, it is right now.

God moved me to publish *Prayer Still Works*, a compilation of some of my most impactful sermons about the power, purpose, and payoff of a strong prayer life. Each section begins with a focal passage of scripture, while the chapters in that section outline key points as we see individuals from the Bible face difficulties and respond to them by turning to God in prayer. The final two sections also include guides on how we can maximize the effectiveness of our prayer lives. It is my sincere desire that you use this book, whether on your own, with your spouse, with your entire family, or with your small group, as a weekly devotional where you draw from the principles of these accounts and apply them to your own life. The genuine prayers of the faithful move mountains of all sizes; let us delve into this work together and watch God do some heavy lifting in our families, our churches, our communities, and our very souls. No matter the obstacle: Prayer. Still. Works.

Section 1:

Give It To God

PRAYER STILL WORKS
Kenneth E. Sullivan, Jr.

1 Samuel 1:8-20, NKJV

8 Then Elkanah her husband said to her, "Hannah, why do you weep? Why do you not eat? And why is your heart grieved? Am I not better to you than ten sons?"

9 So Hannah arose after they had finished eating and drinking in Shiloh. Now Eli the priest, was sitting on the seat by the doorpost of the tabernacle of the Lord.

10 And she was in bitterness of soul and prayed to the Lord and wept in anguish.

11 Then she made a vow and said, "O Lord of hosts, if You will indeed look on the affliction of Your maidservant and remember me, and not forget Your maidservant, but will give Your maidservant a male child, then I will give him to the Lord all the days of his life, and no razor shall come upon his head."

12 And it happened, as she continued praying before the Lord, that Eli watched her mouth.

13 Now Hannah spoke in her heart; only her lips moved, but her voice was not heard. Therefore, Eli thought she was drunk.

14 So Eli said to her, "How long will you be drunk? Put your wine away from you!"

15 And Hannah answered and said, "No, my lord, I am a woman of sorrowful spirit. I have drunk neither wine nor intoxicating drink but have poured out my soul before the Lord.

16 Do not consider your maidservant a wicked woman, for out of the abundance of my complaint and grief I have spoken until now."

17 Then Eli answered and said, "Go in peace, and the God of Israel grant your petition which you have asked of Him."

18 And she said, "Let your maidservant find favor in your sight." So, the woman went her way and ate, and her face was no longer sad.

19 Then they rose early in the morning and worshiped before the Lord and returned and came to their house at Ramah. And Elkanah knew Hannah his wife, and the Lord remembered her.

20 So it came to pass in the process of time that Hannah conceived and bore a son, and called his name Samuel, saying, "Because I have asked for him from the Lord."

There are times in all of our lives when, no matter what we do or how hard we try, we can't seem to get the kind of results we are looking for. We have moments when we find ourselves struggling with things to the point of exhaustion. I want to encourage you to take whatever you are wrestling with or trying to make happen on your own and *Give it to God*. If you are reading this and feeling weighed down by worry, or if you are plagued by pressure or feeling crushed by the concerns you're carrying, I want to encourage you to *Give it to God*.

Jesus will work it out if you let Him! That's what this text is tailored to teach us. We are introduced to a desperate housewife by the name of Hannah. She has a loving husband and a nice house, but she does not have the thing she desires the most.

Have you ever been there? Life overall was pretty good for you, but there is just that one thing that's weighing heavy on you, making it hard for you to enjoy other things?

For example, you have your own house, but it's not a happy home. Or your marriage is good, but your child is struggling in school. Maybe your family is doing well, but your career is not. Or your career is going well, and you also have the house and the car but no one to share it with. You have some good things going, but that one thing has you discouraged, disappointed, and down. In fact, it has you filled with anxiety because you're asking God, "When is it going to happen? How is it going to happen? *Will it ever happen*??" There you are, in anguish, worrying about when your situation will change. That's where Hannah is, and Hannah helps us understand how to handle the heavy stuff that weighs on us and brings us down.

CHAPTER 1

Hannah Requests to Give Birth

Her Desire

Hannah wants to have a baby. Badly. She wants a baby, but scripture says she is barren and unable to, and this is weighing heavily on her. In Old Testament times, a childless woman was considered a failure, and it was embarrassing for a married woman not to have children. A woman gained dignity and found her identity in her children (see Genesis 16:1-5; Genesis 30:1-3). To be barren was a social stigma and an embarrassment for her husband. A woman's success or failure and life meaning were found through motherhood, and there was true pressure to produce offspring. So, the pressure of having a child is heavy on Hannah's heart. She wants her husband to be happy and to overcome this sense of feeling like a failure, but scripture says she was barren, unable to produce.

Have you ever felt barren or had to experience an unproductive period in your life? Maybe at work or in your career or business, perhaps in your search for a mate or in terms of a goal or aim? You are trying to make things happen, but they are just not happening. Perhaps you're trying desperately to be fruitful and productive, but your attempts are unsuccessful. You haven't gotten the results you had hoped for. You only seem to have met with failure. Despite your hard work, nothing seems to be happening for you. You put forth the effort, but you haven't been able to be effective. (It's one thing not to be productive because you're not trying; it's another thing to try and *still* not be productive.) For example, you're working hard at trying to find employment, but you haven't landed an interview, or working hard at trying to get married but with no success in getting a date. Maybe you are working hard to get your sales up or improve your own business but to no avail.

I believe that God allows us to experience unproductive periods because He wants us to learn how to depend on Him. Notice twice in verses 5-6 it says that the Lord had closed Hannah's womb. It's possible that God closed her womb so that she would have to come to Him for things to open up and for her to be productive. God allowed Hannah to be barren and to fail at her attempts to become pregnant so that she would have to seek Him. If her womb was going to open up, it would be a result of God's work.

See, sometimes God brings us to a place where we have to realize that only He can do what we need to be done. God does this so we learn not to trust in ourselves but to trust in Him. Every now and then, God allows us to deal with something that forces us to recognize that if the bill is going to get paid, God is going to have to do it. If the situation is going to change, God is going to have to do it. If the problem is going to be solved, God will have to do it. If the verdict is going to be overruled, God is going to have to do it. If that position is going to open up, God is going to have to do it.

God allows things to be closed to help us understand there are some things only He can open up, some things only He can produce, some things only He can solve, fix, correct, or improve. We must look to Him to do for us what we cannot do for ourselves.

Philippians 4:6-7 says, *"Be anxious for nothing, but in everything by prayer and supplication with thanksgiving let your requests be made known to God. The peace of God will guard you."* Supplication means request, petition, or entreaty and involves asking one in authority for their assistance in a matter or a situation. It involves humbling yourself before them and putting it into their hands.

Sometimes God just wants us to come to Him and say, "Father, I stretch my hand to Thee, no other help I know. If Thou withdraw Thyself from me wither, shall I go?"

Sometimes you can't say a word; sometimes, you can't articulate what you need; all you can do is reach out and groan. God will reach up and give you what you need. He's just waiting for you to get Him involved. He says, "Call unto Me, and I'll answer and give you inaccessible things!" That's what God wants us to do—request His involvement. I believe God closed her womb so that she would have to come to Him and trust Him to open things up for her.

Her Decision

What Hannah wanted was noble, but she could neither achieve it nor obtain it on her own. Hannah shows us how to get from God what we want. In verse 11, she makes a vow to God that if He gives her what she desires, she will dedicate it back to Him.

Hannah may have actually been saying, *"Okay, Lord, I wanted and desired a child for my own selfish reasons, but now I realize that what I want, You want me to have so that I might honor You with it. God, maybe I was selfish and self-centered in what I was seeking, but now I know that You're not just interested in what I want, but what You will get out of what I'm asking You to give me."* See, God doesn't mind us having desires for certain things; in fact, He places those desires in us. God wants our desires to line up with what He desires and for us to align our will with His will. Psalm 37:4 says, "Delight yourself in the Lord, and He will give you the desires of your heart."

God wants to know how you are going to honor Him for giving you what you want. He asks, "What am I going to get out of it? What will I get in return for giving you that job, opening that door, blessing you with that house or car, or giving you that financial increase?" Some of us ask God for things, but we are not concerned with how God will be honored by our getting them. God wants to know what you plan to do for Him once He blesses you. Will you use the new car to come to church and look for other people to load up and bring with you on the way? Will you use the financial increase and invest some of it back into His Kingdom? Will you honor Him in that new house and use it as a means to host and to have others over to show them the love of Christ? Will you be a light in that company if He promotes you to the position you ask for? What's in it for God?

Scripture says you have not because you ask not, and when you ask, you don't receive what you request because you ask amiss or for your own selfish reasons (James 4:2).

When you make your request before God, ask yourself what's in it for God. How does the thing you're looking for line up with what God wants? What will God get out of what you're asking Him to give you? Ask yourself how you can honor God with what you desire; this will help you line up your desires with God's desires. Say, "God, I don't want You just to bless me. I want you to bless others *through* me. I want

You to give it to me so I can give it back to You and use it for Your glory!"

Hannah prayed sincerely, specifically and sacrificially. She made the request, and then she made a release.

CHAPTER 2

Hannah Releases Her Burden

She Puts It In His Hands

Hannah handed over to God the thing that was weighing heavy on her heart. Hannah tells God that the whole matter is now in His hands. She gave what she had to God, which is just what we must do.

I believe that too many of us are carrying things we should not be concerned about. We are weighed down with things we need not be worried about. We have allowed things to steal our peace and joy and keep us up at night, things we keep turning over in our minds that fill us with anxiety and stress. We often forfeit peace and bear needless pains because we do not go to God in prayer. Certain things were designed for us to do, but then there are certain things God wants us to give to Him and allow Him to take care of. You have to know the difference between what you can handle and what you must give to God to handle.

At the airport, there are baggage checkpoints where they check your bags, weigh your bags, and determine whether or not your bag is considered a carry-on or something you need to give to them and allow them to handle. They do not allow you to carry on bags that are too large or too heavy because there is no room for them on the aircraft, and it is not good for you or the other passengers. Sometimes I've been disappointed when I've attempted to carry on a bag that I considered small enough for me to carry, and then they say, "Sir, we are sorry, but you can't carry that on, and you're going to have to check it." Each time I turn it over to them with frustration, but I get on the plane, and I'm good. Their intervention makes traveling easier, and I do not have to worry about wrestling with it, bumping into people, and offending people with my bags.

Some of us are going through life carrying too much baggage. We are weighed down with worry, bogged down with burdens, and struggling with stress. God did not intend for you to carry some of the stuff you're carrying and to carry on the way that you are, consistently worried and stressed out. He said to cast all your cares upon Him because He cares about you (1 Peter 5:7). God declares that He cares about your children, He cares about your health, He cares about your job, He cares about you getting a good night's sleep, and He cares about every hair on your head.

God wants you to take all the stuff that keeps you up at night—stuff that's robbing you of your peace and joy, that's causing you to bite your fingernails, that's filling you up with anxiety and fear and worry, and take that off your shoulders and release it completely to Him. Put it all in His hands!

Put it in God's hands because He can handle whatever you don't have a handle on. When you put your problems in God's hands, God will put His peace in your heart. Realize that God already knows what we ask before we even ask (Matthew 6:8). God knows your thoughts from afar off. He knows your rising up from your sitting down. God knows you so well that when you can't even fix your mouth to say it, He will answer. Notice Hannah prays without speaking; she's moving her mouth, but she's not praying aloud, and God still heard her and understood what she was saying as she poured her heart out to the Father.

She Pours Out Her Heart

Hannah's prayer is one of the most passionate and intimate prayers presented in the Bible. We see Hannah's heart and soul poured out on the altar before God. Prayer is the highest level of intimacy a person can have with God. It's all of who you are connecting with all of who God is. It's an intimate act.

When you are intimate with someone, you take off what you are wearing and allow them to see and share your private areas. You expose yourself to them and make yourself vulnerable. Similarly, when we pray, we open ourselves up entirely to God and allow Him to see our private areas. The stuff we can't show or tell everybody, the parts of ourselves we keep concealed, we reveal to God in prayer.

So, when we open up in prayer, we are exposing ourselves completely to God. We allow Him to see and share the stuff we don't feel comfortable allowing any and everybody to see and share. See, some things you can't share with everybody, and sometimes you can't say how you really feel for fear of people taking you the wrong way and misunderstanding where you are coming from, possibly judging you, or just making you feel bad. But with God, you can feel comfortable coming to Him and sharing with Him your private parts, your faults, and all of your secret thoughts. You can tell God how you feel, what's on your mind, and what's going on with you. You can feel comfortable being naked before God. You don't have to worry about Him misinterpreting what you're trying to say or taking it the wrong way. God wants us to confide in Him, to share with Him the stuff that causes us to struggle. Scripture says that as a father pities his children, so God pities us. He knows how we were made and remembers that we are dust (Psalm 103:13-14).

Notice scripture says Hannah is pouring out her soul before God. She gave it all to God; she didn't hold anything back. Hannah came to the house of the Lord to connect with God. Verses 4,10 and 19 tell us Hannah is at church to pray and worship. She is concentrating on God, giving Him her all. Hannah is acknowledging God. She is weeping and praying and worshipping her Lord, pouring herself out before Him and giving Him the best that she's got—mind, body, and soul.

In the middle of her intimate time with God, Hannah is misjudged. Eli misjudges her and misunderstands what she is doing in worship. Now, he is the priest, and he misjudges her worship and her sincerity. You would think this is someone who should be more sensitive to the Spirit and attuned to what's happening in worship, but he's not. Some of us, even leaders in the church, can misjudge people who are sincerely worshipping. We can question their purity and sincerity. If we are not careful, we can become so insulated in the house of worship that we can no longer identify with those who come and engage in true worship.

See, some people in the church do not understand and cannot comprehend authentic worship and true devotion. They have a hard time understanding why you lift your hands, open your mouth, and wave your hand. They don't know why, even though you have problems, you can give

God praise the way you do. They don't see the rationale behind it all. Some, in fact, think you are crazy or that *"it doesn't take all that."*

In Hannah's case, Eli thought she was drunk. This was the same mistake some made on the Day of Pentecost after the Holy Ghost had fallen and the disciples started speaking in ways they had not heard before (Acts 2). Hannah told Eli that she knew he might not understand her worship and devotion and her reason for doing what she was doing in the sanctuary. She let him know that he did not know her story and what she had been going through to that point. He did not understand her pain and misjudged her. Her worship was for real. Eli did not know what she was experiencing nor what Hannah was expecting and looking for God to do in her life. She was crying and lifting her hands and moving her lips because her heart was ready to receive a blessing from God!

CHAPTER 3

Hannah Receives Her Blessing

She Gave It To God; God Gave It To her

God gave Hannah what she asked of Him because she gave it all over to Him. Scripture says that after she finished praying and spent time in worship, Hannah returned home and soon became pregnant (verses 19-20). This was no artificial insemination. This was *supernatural* insemination. The Lord remembered Hannah and opened her womb and caused her to conceive. This was God's way of rewarding her for giving Him all of her. See, when you seek after God, you will receive supernatural responses. Scripture says that God is a rewarder of those who diligently seek after Him (Hebrews 11:6).

Notice the entire time Hannah had been married, she couldn't get pregnant. Before, she had been intimate with her husband, but they could not produce; she became pregnant when she gave it to God. She could not conceive for all that time, but she received her reward after giving it to God in worship. We see here that Hannah's intimacy with God *improved* her intimacy with her husband. God did something new between her and her husband in the bedroom *after* she had prayed and worshipped. God can do some stuff through worship and devotion that can't be done in the human connection alone. God can do some things with *you* that nobody else can do; He can touch you in places nobody else can, make you feel like nobody else can, and fulfill you as nobody else can. Can't nobody do you like Jesus! It all happened in worship!

Hannah came to church heavy, but she left happy. She came in distressed, but she left delighted. She came in low, but she left with her spirit lifted. She came in carrying a burden, but she left carrying a blessing. It happened in worship!

I believe that God has a blessing for you. But some of us are not getting the stuff we are looking for from God because we are unwilling to give it all to God. We are unwilling to really get out of ourselves and worship Him in spirit and truth (John 4:23). If you learn how to forget about yourself and concentrate on Him, God can truly bless you! If you learn to delight yourself in the Lord, He will give you the desires of your heart! (Psalm 37:4) If you give it all to Him without worrying about who is looking and who sees you, I believe God will begin to bless you and start opening up some stuff that's been closed. I don't know about you, but I'm not worried about what people may think or say about my connection to God when I worship. I need too much from God.

I'm looking for God to do too much; I need some stuff to open up that's been closed; I need some stuff to break. I'm trying to get pregnant. Pregnant with promise. Pregnant with blessings. Pregnant with new vision. Pregnant with God's possibilities. So, my hands are lifted. My lips are moving. My heart is ready to receive a blessing from heaven! Do you feel the same way I do? When you enter into worship, I dare you to forget about who may be looking and say, "Lord, I need a touch. Lord, I need a miracle. Lord, I need a breakthrough! My hands are lifted, and my heart is ready to receive! I'm giving You my burdens. I'm giving You my worries. I'm giving You the praise and glory for it already having been done!" Try Him; if you give God what He deserves, God will provide you with what you desire!

When I was growing up, gas stations did not require prepay. You could get your gas and then, afterward, pay the attendant what you owed. But, people abused that—they were getting gas but would just drive away and not pay like they were supposed to. So, they changed that and made it a requirement to pay in advance before releasing the resources. Many of us have gotten from God what we desire, but we haven't given God what He deserves. So, God now says that before He releases specific blessings, resources, and things you want, He needs you to praise Him in advance. Despite your current situation, God needs you to give Him the praise He deserves, the honor He deserves, and the worship He is due! For just a moment, give God some praise right where you are. When praise goes up, blessings start flowing! Give it to God, and He will give it to you!

Section 2:

PUSH (Pray Until Something Happens)

2 Kings 19:1-4, 14-20

1 And so it was, when King Hezekiah heard it, that he tore his clothes, covered himself with sackcloth, and went into the house of the Lord.

2 Then he sent Eliakim, who was over the household, Shebna the scribe, and the elders of the priests, covered with sackcloth, to Isaiah the prophet, the son of Amoz.

3 And they said to him, "Thus says Hezekiah: 'This day is a day of trouble, and rebuke, and blasphemy; for the children have come to birth, but there is no strength to [a]bring them forth.

4 It may be that the Lord your God will hear all the words of the Rabshakeh, whom his master the king of Assyria has sent to reproach the living God, and will rebuke the words which the Lord your God has heard. Therefore lift up your prayer for the remnant that is left.' "

14 And Hezekiah received the letter from the hand of the messengers, and read it; and Hezekiah went up to the house of the Lord, and spread it before the Lord.

15 Then Hezekiah prayed before the Lord, and said: "O Lord God of Israel, the One who dwells between the cherubim, You are God, You alone, of all the kingdoms of the earth. You have made heaven and earth.

16 *Incline Your ear, O Lord, and hear; open Your eyes, O Lord, and see; and hear the words of Sennacherib, which he has sent to reproach the living God.*

17 *Truly, Lord, the kings of Assyria have laid waste the nations and their lands,*

18 *And have cast their gods into the fire; for they were not gods, but the work of men's hands – wood and stone. Therefore they destroyed them.*

19 *Now therefore, O Lord our God, I pray, save us from his hand, that all the kingdoms of the earth may know that You are the Lord God, You alone."*

20 *Then Isaiah the son of Amoz sent to Hezekiah, saying, "Thus says the Lord God of Israel: 'Because you have prayed to Me against Sennacherib king of Assyria, I have heard.'*

Every now and then, life confronts us with challenges that are too overwhelming for us to overcome in our own strength. Sometimes we find ourselves forced to deal with human emergencies that require divine intervention. Are you standing in need of a breakthrough? Are you in need of an answer or need some assistance? If that is you and you're going to get the deliverance you need, you're going to have to PUSH.

This is what Hezekiah learned, and it served him well for the rest of his life. You will find that Hezekiah was a praying man who learned how to pray in and through a crisis. Then, in the next chapter, he receives some more bad news, but he prays until God turns things around and extends his life. It was the crisis in this chapter of his life that really taught Hezekiah how to pray.

At this time, Assyria is the only world superpower. The Assyrians had conquered several neighboring nations and forced them to pay them tribute; Judah is one of those nations. In the 14th year of his reign, after some encouragement by the ruler in Egypt, Hezekiah decides to skip payment and rebel against Assyria. The Assyrian King, Sennacherib, responded by surrounding Jerusalem and besieging forty of Israel's fortified cities. Now faced with the backlash of failure to pay, Hezekiah agrees to pay the tribute with interest. He strips his royal palace of its gold and silver and precious articles. He taps into the temple treasury and uses some of its articles in an attempt to appease Sennacherib, but this is not enough.

Sennacherib was determined to make an example out of Hezekiah and Judah lest other nations controlled by Assyria get the idea of skipping payment. He sends a delegation to the wall near the palace of King Hezekiah to negotiate terms of surrender. He sends one of his chief officers, his Field Commander, his Secretary of State, and his head General of the Army, and scripture says he also sent "a great army" to the door of King Hezekiah (2 Kings 18:17). This was a very impressive and intimidating show of force. In fact, it's described as "a day of distress." (2 Kings 19:3) Distress is defined as pain or suffering affecting the body or the mind or a state of danger or desperate need. It is a condition requiring immediate help.

CHAPTER 4

Hezekiah's Distress

Day Of Distress For The King, Nation, And People

Hezekiah and the people are terrified and with good reason. Rabshakeh tells him to surrender, that resistance is futile, and all other nations who've attempted defiance have failed. There is no point in prolonging the inevitable defeat. This was a dark day for Judah, indeed; it was a day of distress.

The threat from the Assyrian king comes as an announcement before Judah for all of the people to hear. The Field Commander speaks to Hezekiah's representatives while in a very public place. As a matter of fact, Eliakim, the son of Hezekiah's administrator, asks him not to speak so loud and to speak in Aramaic so that only Hezekiah's messengers could understand instead of everyone who was around, since they may become afraid. Rabshakeh responds by speaking longer and louder in everyone's language (Hebrew) so that all can hear the disheartening words.

They are told that Judah's situation is hopeless, that they can't believe God will help them because all other neighboring countries have been conquered, and God never helped any of them. They are told there's no hope, that they might as well give up and surrender, using the statistics and stories of others who've already succumbed to paint a bleak picture. Rabshakeh says they'll lose their homes, eat dung, and be destroyed, and he broadcasts the message to frighten the people.

They hear these stories, they see this intimidating show of force, and it leaves the people filled with fear, feeling as though they are facing an uncertain future. The people are in distress due to the bad report they've just received.

One of the tactics of the enemy is fear and intimidation. He likes to present disheartening stories and scenarios about others and then tell you that's the same stuff that will happen to you. He likes to forward and deposit and send bad news into your spirit so that you become fearful and frightened about your future. He wants to disturb you, disrupt your peace, and fill you with fear.

That's why you have to guard your heart, for out of it flows the issues of life (Proverbs 4:23). Guard your heart and mind against the stuff that will fill you with fear and distress. Don't answer some of those calls, don't reply to some of those texts, and ignore some of those emails. Some messages don't need your attention—do not listen or respond.

Some stuff is just spam sent from Satan, designed to scare you and shut you down. If you open it up, it will mess you up. It will shut down your systems, make it hard for you to operate, and ruin your "good files."

You have to be careful where you get your news and what broadcasts you listen to. Some of the news is depressing, and it can sap your faith and your joy. It can even make you pessimistic and afraid to go outside, to work, and live life. By the time you finish listening, they'll have you thinking you're going to lose your job, your house, your health, and your mind.

Some of the people in the news are fear-mongers who exaggerate and exasperate problems or situations. Many of them are atheists or agnostic, pessimistic people who see things differently than people of God. Remember, Hezekiah, that Rabshakeh doesn't believe in your God, and he has a different perspective on things. So, when he brings or bears bad news, that news is not even meant for you. The mail he is delivering may have been meant for someone else.

All kinds of mail comes to my house every day. Sometimes I see the bills and the mail from unfamiliar places, and I have to say, "Wait a minute, that's not for me. That's the wrong address—it's for somebody else." Sometimes the enemy sends you a message and mail that's not intended for you to receive. Don't open it, don't entertain it, don't receive it; mark that "return to sender" or "wrong address." Let the sender know that you don't accept that your child won't succeed, or that you'll die of this disease, or that you're going to lose what you have been blessed to gain. Tell the devil that he has the wrong address, and this mail is for somebody else! You dwell at 91st and Psalm Street, in the secret place of the Most High and under the shadow of the Almighty. The Lord is your refuge and fortress, and He says you don't have to be afraid of the arrow that flies by day nor the pestilence that walks at night or destruction that lays waste at noonday. He said 1,000 may fall at your side and 10,000 by your right hand, but it wouldn't come near your dwelling. Say to the enemy, "This is not my mail! I'm sending it back to hell where it came from! No, my mail reads I'm blessed and highly favored! I'm the head and not the tail! I'm the righteousness of God. I'm the Seed of Abraham! Check your address!!"

Bad News Has Broken Hezekiah's Spirit

Hezekiah is in distress because Judah needs to be delivered from a difficult circumstance, and he can't deliver them. Hezekiah is now forced to face his own human limitations. Here is a King who is used to figuring things out, fixing things, and resolving issues. He's the leader, and the people look to him to solve problems and make things right. But

Hezekiah is forced to admit that the problem he and the nation face he cannot fix. Hezekiah has to realize that he doesn't have the resources to rectify the situation on his own.

Every now and then, life will hand you a reminder that your resources are not adequate to answer all of your problems. I don't know if you've been faced with a situation that you have no power over and are forced to face your own human limitations and recognize that you don't have the answers to your problems and what you need to be done you can't do. You're at a loss for words, your resources are exhausted, and you have no answers.

Have you ever tried to settle a situation only to have it respond to you and say *Declined*? You have insufficient resources and don't have what it takes to complete and cover this transaction. Sometimes a problem will speak back and let you know that you can't pay your way out of it, think your way out of it, scheme your way out of it, manipulate or negotiate your way out of it; all you can do is pray your way out of it.

There is some stuff college did not prepare you for, and some stuff friends and family can't fix. These are things only God can solve, and the only way they will be worked out is if God gets involved. If the bill is going to get paid, God will have to pay it. If you are going to walk through that door,

God will have to open it. If the situation is going to change, God will have to change it.

When you realize your resources are insufficient, you've got to reach up for divine intervention. I remember working out of a building years ago that went through a rezoning process. I had to attend a hearing and then wait for others to decide whether I could continue to operate my business in that space. There was nothing I could do. I couldn't change it. I couldn't rush it. I couldn't even hide it. They posted a letter in public view stating that a court would decide the outcome. I was shaken and powerless, and in my powerlessness, I had no choice but to pray. It was my problem that pushed me to really pray. That problem produced prayers in me I had never prayed. In fact, my greatest problems have produced some of my greatest prayers! Could it be that some of the issues we are plagued with are designed to push us to pray? If I never had a problem, I wouldn't know God could solve them. Real problems produce real prayers. Serious problems produce serious prayers, and the more complex the problems, the deeper the prayers.

This is where Hezekiah finds himself in this passage. He is at a place where he is powerless and defenseless. He is without strength. Note how he describes himself and his situation in chapter 19, verse 3. He compares himself to a woman in the delivery room at the point of giving birth but unable to do so. For a powerful king to liken himself and his situation to that of a woman struggling to give birth demonstrates just how powerless he views himself and the situation. Clearly, the king and nation are in turmoil. It is a day of distress.

CHAPTER 5

Hezekiah's Decision

Hezekiah Seeks Godly Counsel In A Time Of Crisis

Hezekiah didn't call for his Secretary of Defense. He didn't call his Secretary of Foreign Affairs or his Head of National Security. Instead, he called on Eliakim, Shebna, Joah, and the elders and priests. These men are senior religious leaders in the temple, and Hezekiah sends them, covered in sackcloth, to the prophet Isaiah. They have instructions to ask Isaiah to pray.

Remember how Hezekiah describes his situation, like that of a woman struggling to give birth. To continue the illustration, we might say that he surrounds himself with men who act as spiritual midwives. Before there were OB/GYNs, there were midwives who assisted women in childbirth to help bring about delivery. In the first chapter of Exodus, Pharaoh told the midwives to kill the Hebrew males when they were born in his attempt to suppress population growth as Israel was growing too numerous. But scripture says the midwives feared God and did not follow the decree. They helped bring about the deliverance of many and strengthen the nation (Exodus 1:17-20).

That's what our nation needs — some spiritual midwives. We need some midwives, some people who will cry out to God for the nation and stand in the gap for our people. In 2 Chronicles 7:14, God says, *"If My people who are called by My name will humble themselves and pray, and seek My face, and turn from their wicked ways, then will I hear from Heaven, forgive their sins, and heal their land."* We need some midwives to facilitate a spiritual delivery for this country. See, when you've got a personal crisis and need a breakthrough, you don't need folks just standing by talking and speculating; you need folks who are in tune with God. You need folks who know how to get a prayer through. I don't need meddlers. I need some midwives.

Yeah, I need some folks who aren't afraid to help out in the delivery room. I know it's gory; I know it's unpleasant; I know everybody can't handle it; I know not everybody has the stomach for it, but I need some folks who can help me *PUSH*. I need some folks who can give me a word of knowledge and who will encourage my soul. I need some folks who will touch and agree with me to hold my hand in the delivery room while I *PUSH* to give birth to what God has designed for me.

After receiving Hezekiah's request for prayer, Isaiah sends word back to him, urging him not to be afraid. Isaiah tells Hezekiah that a rumor will cause Sennacherib to return to his own country, and God will use the distraction to defeat the Assyrian king. Hezekiah experienced a moment of relief after receiving the word from the prophet. Still, Sennacherib sends another message to Hezekiah, reminding him of the strength of the Assyrian army, all of the success they've had in war, and that Hezekiah cannot trust God to deliver him just like those other nations could not trust their gods to deliver them. Hezekiah's relief is short-lived, and he is again shaken. But, after receiving the letter, Hezekiah goes off by himself to pray. He went to the temple, spread out the pages of the letter, and talked to God about what was on his heart. When Hezekiah didn't know what else to do, he took it to the Lord in prayer.

While it's good to have support from others, and it's important to have prayer warriors on your side, you've got to know how to call on God for yourself. Nobody can express to God what you're going through better than you can. Nobody can tell God exactly what you need better than you can. If you're going to get your breakthrough, you're going to have to *PUSH*.

I notice in the delivery room that while there may be family, nurses, and doctors assisting, it's up to the one giving birth to put forth an effort to bring about the delivery. In the same way, when it comes to issues you face, you must put forth the effort to seek God for yourself. You're going to have to *PUSH*. That means you're going to have to exert some energy and put forth some effort to get the deliverance or breakthrough you need. You've got to learn to get by yourself and encourage yourself. You must push yourself, lay hands on yourself, and build yourself up in your most holy faith while praying in the spirit to the only one who can answer in the way that you need.

Do you know how to pray for yourself? Do you know how to get before God on your face and not get up until you get through and get an answer from Him? This is so critical because the secret is nobody can pray for you. Nobody can speak for you like you can. Nobody. Sometimes God is saying, "Speak up and call me for yourself! I want to hear from YOU! I want to hear your voice and your prayers, and your petitions directly from your heart. I need for you to call Me on your behalf."

The Bible gives us plenty of examples of men and women who reached out to God for themselves to get their breakthroughs. Blind Bartimaeus cried out and got Jesus' attention for himself to receive his healing (Mark 10:46-52). The woman with the issue of blood pressed and pushed her way through a crowd until she got to Jesus and received some of His power (Luke 8:43-48). If you really want to get a response from God, sometimes He wants to hear directly from *you*. He doesn't want co-signers. He wants to know if you can carry this thing to Him yourself. It's as if God said to Hezekiah, "I know you're a king and you're used to delegating and having other people speak for you and buffer for you and carry out things for you; but, King, if you're going to get a breakthrough this time, you can't delegate prayer — you've got to learn how to do it for yourself!"

Leaders know that there are certain tasks they can't delegate to others. It's not that they don't have capable people on their team, but some tasks just have to be completed by the boss to get the best outcome. Nobody can articulate to God what you need the way that you can. You've got to *PUSH*!

CHAPTER 6

Hezekiah's Delivery

Hezekiah Takes the Letter to Church

I like the fact that, while Hezekiah was going through this challenging time, he took his problem to the house of God. He didn't run *from* the church. He ran *to* the church. When you're going through and need a breakthrough, it's important that you get to the church to get your deliverance. The church is the delivery room where you can get the support you need to *PUSH*.

Hezekiah takes the threatening letter that he's received and literally lays it out before God. Whenever you get a bad report or some bad news, take it before the Lord and spread it out. Ask God to speak to it.

Every January, I lead our church in a 21-day fast. As one component of this special time of consecration and rededication, we open up the sanctuary for prayer at noon every day. I challenge the disciples to bring any and every concern they have to the altar in prayer. Bring the disconnect notice, the doctor's report or bill, the court summons, that child's report card, the pink slip—bring it all, and lay it before the Lord our God. He sees, He knows, and He will answer that prayer.

Hezekiah pushes his way into the temple, and he prays. This is no easy prayer; Hezekiah gets to the altar before the Lord and pours himself out. This is a prayer filled with emotions, tears, and cries. Hezekiah's prayer is agonizing; it's intense, time-consuming, and draining. This prayer contains the same pain and emotions that one may experience in a delivery room during a difficult childbirth.

There is sheer emotion in the delivery room. There's discomfort, even moments of anguish. Some deliveries are more intense, take longer, and require more effort, energy, and exertion than others. Sometimes the mother has to push for extended periods to receive that precious gift God has for her.

My sister told me that she was in labor for three days to deliver her second son. She shared how she had to get up and walk at different intervals, that she would get sick and that she vomited more than once, that she had to push and push and stop and wait and go through these exercises then try again. She felt at times that she was going to go insane as she struggled to deliver him.

Some situations we face in life require more prayer and effort than others. We pray about some issues and things we face or carry, and God seems to work it out rather quickly. But then there are certain things we face in life that require a lot more effort in prayer, fasting, and seeking God. For some issues, we have to labor, like difficult childbirth. Sometimes it may take a few minutes, sometimes a few hours, sometimes a few days. Sometimes you're going to have to get down on your face and not get up until you get through and hear your answer from God.

There is also some opposition you'll face, some trials you'll endure, some issues you'll encounter, some stubborn sins, strongholds, challenges, or struggles you'll face that will require you to push back the plate and fast while you pray. In Mark 9:29, Jesus says that certain demons only go out by prayer and fasting. In Daniel chapter 9, scripture says that Daniel, the prophet, fasted and prayed, seeking to hear from God and receive revelation. During his time of prayer, the angel Gabriel showed up and gave Daniel a message from God. God said that since Daniel set his heart to seek God, He purposed to send Daniel a delivery, but the prince of Persia was trying to block the breakthrough. Michael, the Archangel, was sent to aid Gabriel and free him up to bring

Daniel this special delivery, and Daniel was able to receive the prophecy concerning things to come. Daniel got his breakthrough because he kept on pushing. I believe there are some things God wants to give us, but we're going to have to *PUSH*. We miss some things because we don't *PUSH* hard enough. When you fast, don't do it just to drop a few pounds; no -- fast and pray and target those issues that you're dealing with. Say, *"God, I need a breakthrough! At the end of this, I want to see You more clearly. I want to be more like You. God, I pray that you break some stuff in my life, reveal Yourself, Father God!!" PUSH!!*

We don't know how long it took for Hezekiah to pray until God answered, but he prayed until something happened. He prayed until he got delivery. Notice that God speaks and sends a word to Hezekiah by the prophet Isaiah. God pronounced judgment on Assyria, and in one night, God struck down 185,000 Assyrians while they lay asleep in their tents. Sennacherib fled back home. Judah was delivered. Hezekiah prayed, *and something happened*!

Whatever problem you have—*PUSH!* Whatever opposition you're facing—*PUSH!* Whatever crisis you have—*PUSH!* Whatever issue you're dealing with—*PUSH!* I know you're tired, but *PUSH!* I know you're frustrated, but *PUSH!* I know it gets discouraging, and it doesn't seem like it's getting any better, but *PUSH!* I know you've prayed already but keep on, like never before—*PUSH!*

Pray in the morning. Pray in the noonday. Pray in the midnight hour. Pray until depression leaves. Pray until things change. Pray until you get your breakthrough. Pray until you get your healing. Pray until you get your answer. Pray until you get deliverance. Pray. Until. Something. Happens!!

Section 3:

God Will Turn It Around

2 Kings 20:1-11

1 In those days Hezekiah was sick and near death. And Isaiah the prophet, the son of Amoz, went to him and said to him, "Thus says the Lord: 'Set your house in order, for you shall die, and not live.'"

2 Then he turned his face toward the wall, and prayed to the Lord, saying,

3 "Remember now, O Lord, I pray, how I have walked before You in truth and with a loyal heart, and have done what was good in Your sight." And Hezekiah wept bitterly.

4 And it happened, before Isaiah had gone out into the middle court, that the word of the Lord came to him, saying,

5 "Return and tell Hezekiah the leader of My people, 'Thus says the Lord, the God of David your father: "I have heard your prayer, I have seen your tears; surely I will heal you. On the third day you shall go up to the house of the Lord.

6 And I will add to your days fifteen years. I will deliver you and this city from the hand of the king of Assyria; and I will defend this city for My own sake, and for the sake of My servant David."

7 Then Isaiah said, "Take a lump of figs." So they took and laid it on the boil, and he recovered.

8 And Hezekiah said to Isaiah, "What is the sign that the Lord will heal me, and that I shall go up to the house of the Lord the third day?"

9 Then Isaiah said, "This is the sign to you from the Lord, that the Lord will do the thing which He has spoken: shall the shadow go forward ten degrees or go backward ten degrees?"

10 And Hezekiah answered, "It is an easy thing for the shadow to go down ten degrees; no, but let the shadow go backward ten degrees."

11 So Isaiah the prophet cried out to the Lord, and He brought the shadow ten degrees backward, by which it had gone down on the sundial of Ahaz.

Have you ever found yourself at a place where you needed something changed or fixed in your life, but you didn't have the power to do it? Have you ever found yourself dealing with something that seemed to be immovable or incurable? Every now and then, we find ourselves facing what appears to be an irreversible situation, and we don't know which way to turn.

I believe that God allows us to deal with these kinds of situations to remind us that He alone has the power to reverse what is seemingly irreversible. We must realize that God can turn it around no matter how bad or bleak the situation. It's not over until God says it's over.

For 100 years, Hezekiah is the only faithful king in Judah. He brought in social reforms and spiritual revival. He removed the gods of the Assyrians, he purified the temple, and he stopped paying tribute to the King of Assyria. He opened the doors to the house of the Lord and implemented priestly service and worship again. He worked to remove idolatry and bring true worship back to Judah. In the books of Kings and Chronicles, there is as much coverage given to Hezekiah as there is to King Solomon.

When Hezekiah was 39 years old, having served as king for 14 years, he received some startling and disturbing news. He finds himself facing a situation he can't solve, and he can't reverse...But God.

CHAPTER 7

The Report for Hezekiah

He Must Have Practical Faith

Hezekiah contracts a severe disease, and he takes ill. He is told he is going to die. Here was a man who had followed God faithfully for his entire life, yet he received some unfortunate news and had to deal with sickness and trouble. This is not supposed to happen to a man who has lived a holy life. How can you serve God and still deal with difficulty? Some of us think we are not supposed to receive bad news or deal with troubling situations because we serve God faithfully. But I want to help clarify something for you: you must understand that you can live right, work hard, be faithful to God, serve in the church, pay your tithes, treat others with love and respect, and still find yourself dealing with difficulties. You can be a Christian and still deal with a crisis. You can be holy and still suffer heartache. You can love Jesus and still lose your job. You can be a saint and still get sick. You can be a disciple and still experience death or destruction.

As we read in Psalm 34:19, *"Many afflictions suffer the righteous, but the Lord delivers us out of them all."* Pain, suffering, trials, and disappointment are not discriminatory— they affect us all. None of us are exempt from dealing with trouble, hardships, sickness, job loss, or tragedy. It has nothing to do with whether or not God loves you; it's called LIFE. *"Man, born of woman, lives but a few days and they are full of trouble."* (Job 14:1)

Jesus never promised us we wouldn't have problems; He promised us that, with Him, we would have a partner to help us deal with them. *"In this world, you will have tribulation; but be of good cheer, I have overcome the world."* (John 16:33) Having God doesn't mean trouble won't come; it means you have someone to help carry you through the trouble.

Hezekiah is sick, and Isaiah comes to visit him. Isaiah tells him he is going to die. He drops a bombshell on Hezekiah while he's sick in bed. He tells Hezekiah to make necessary arrangements and to get his estate and personal affairs in order because the end of his life is here. Isaiah didn't say, "Cheer up! Things will get better!" No, he told Hezekiah that he was going to die. Hezekiah was probably expecting to hear some good news from Isaiah because the prophet always brought an encouraging word, but this time he dropped this gut-wrenching news on him. These were not the words of the doctor; this was the word from God. Right then, everything Hezekiah believed about God was put to the test. That's where Hezekiah is at this moment.

And that might be where you are as you are reading this chapter. Everything you thought you knew about God is being tested right now. You're wondering what's really going on and why God is allowing this to happen to you. You might be asking, "God, out of all people, why am I the one who has to go through this?" This might not be the way you expected things to turn out and the answers you are getting have you thrown. Like Hezekiah, you may hear words you were not expecting to hear.

Sometimes we are in situations where our faith is put to the test. See, faith isn't just something you can have in theory; it must be proven in a practical sense. God says faith that cannot be tested is faith that cannot be trusted. So, sometimes God tests our faith.

When I was 16 years old, I was anxious to get my driver's permit. I studied the book from cover to cover. I went to the BMV at 30th and Keystone on the east side of Indianapolis to take my test. First, there was the written exam which I took, and I passed. But then they paired me with a person who would ride in the car with me for the final test. See, they didn't just want to know whether or not I knew the material well enough to explain and answer the questions; they wanted to see if I could handle myself in a practical sense behind the wheel. I only got my permit because I passed both the written *and* the practical driving test.

Faith in God is not just quoting scripture, singing praise songs, or posting faith-filled words on social media. It's more than knowing the proper response and answers to questions posed in the church. Faith is not just theory. It's practical. See, we sing songs that say Jehovah Jireh is my provider, healer, and Way Maker. God says, "Okay, you do well on the written and the verbal portion of the test. How about the practical? Let's get in and see how you do when the rubber meets the road." God wants to see how you do "in traffic" when you have to take unexpected twists and turns, when you have to slam on the brakes, when surprises come from your blind side.

God wants to know if you believe He is a Healer when you get sick or a Waymaker when you see no way out, or that He is a Miracle Worker and a Protector when you are under attack. He does not just want you studying the book to answer questions; He wants to know how you respond to life's difficulties and disappointing news, or lack, threat, sickness, joblessness, and dismay. He wants to see how you respond when the rubber meets the rocky, bumpy, unpaved, uncomfortable road.

He Must Have Personal Faith

Here is Hezekiah's pastor telling him his situation can't be resolved. He states that it can't be changed, and Hezekiah is going to die and not live. What do you do when the doctor's diagnosis is dire, the proven professional's prognosis is not promising, or when the pastor doesn't have anything positive to say about your situation? What do you do when the one you depend on to help, advise, comfort, and bring good news from God can't deliver? What do you do when the people of faith that you depend on don't have faith for your situation to be turned around? That's when you have faith in God for yourself. Some stuff you have to learn to believe for yourself. It's cool that the pastor, elders, prayer partners, and friends can touch and agree with you. But sometimes, the pastor might not see it, your prayer partner might not see it, and your loved ones can't feel it. It's for this very reason that you have to have faith for yourself.

It's during the difficult moments we face that we demonstrate the quality of our faith. Faith is not lip service; faith is a lifestyle. As scripture says, *"The just shall live by faith"* (Hebrews 10:38). It means that righteous people operate by faith. They walk and talk by faith, not by sight. See, sometimes all you might have is faith. You might not have money, health insurance, a job, or rich friends. But do you have faith? Sometimes the situation you find yourself in may not look good or sound good or feel good, but you have to have faith enough in God for yourself to believe He can turn it around. As David said, *"I would've fainted unless I believed that I'd see the goodness of the Lord in the land of the living"* (Psalm 27:13).

Sometimes when Jesus would heal people, their friends would carry them to Him, and they were healed by their friends' faith. But most of the time, when Jesus healed people, He would say, *"Your* faith has made you well" (Matthew 9:22, emphasis added). If your stuff is going to change and turn around, it will require you to have faith.

A well-known, Grammy award-winning gospel artist found herself in a fight for her life after being given a grim report from the doctor about her chances of beating the illness she faced. While in recovery after routine surgery, she began to have trouble breathing. Later they realized she had a blood clot on her lungs, which was traveling toward her heart. She went into a coma and was given just a two percent chance to live. But she believed in the God she had sung about for years. She believed God for herself, despite what her doctors were saying. This woman of God not only came through that season, surgery, and situation healthier and stronger than ever but went on to produce some of her greatest work to date. You have to believe for yourself what God can do, even when nobody else will. You have to have hope even when others have no hope. Remember, it might not be a problem you're facing; the difficulty you're dealing with is going to give God the chance to manufacture your miracle!

Take a moment to repeat these words out loud: *"My Miracle Is In The Making!"*

God is going to use the malady as a means of making your miracle. He's using the trouble to bring about your triumph. He's letting you deal with the confusion so you can see Him calm the storm. What Hezekiah was facing was designed to deepen his faith.

Through it all, thank God for the mountains, the valleys, and the storms He has brought you through. For this reason, you know that He is able and what faith in Him can do.

Do you still believe God is all-powerful and in complete control? Do you believe He can turn situations around? Do you believe in a God who can work wonders even while you wonder how it can work? Do you believe??

CHAPTER 8

The Resolve of Hezekiah

He Recognized His Dependence On God

Hezekiah decided to seek after God and devote his time to prayer. Notice he turned to the wall and sought after God. He didn't turn to his friends. He didn't even call a doctor for a second opinion. He took what he had to God. See, God should be the first person we call when we find ourselves up against a wall. We can hear from everybody else, but most importantly, we need to hear from God.

Hezekiah finds himself up against a wall. His wealth couldn't purchase his health, and neither his strategy, negotiating skills, or degrees could get him out of this one. He found himself at a place where the only person he could turn to was God. Sometimes we find ourselves forced to face situations where nothing else and no one else can help us but God, and God is the only one who can fix it, solve it, change it, reverse it, pay it, or cure it. Sometimes God will allow us to see just how frail we are, how vulnerable we are, how insufficient and incapable we are. He will show us just how much we need Him. God may bring us to our knees so that we learn not to trust in ourselves but in Him. God has a way of causing us to pray and giving us reasons to reach up and reach out to Him to express our dependence on Him. God designs the difficulties in your life to decrease your independence and increase your reliance on Him.

Hezekiah's difficulty, dilemma, and disease were designed to deepen his devotion. The problem was designed to put him in a posture of prayer. (Note: Real problems have a way of producing real prayers!) You haven't *really* prayed until your child is sick, battling drug addiction, or in trouble with the law. You haven't *really* prayed until your heart is broken and your marriage needs to be fixed. You haven't *really* prayed until your bills are overdue, your account is overdrawn, and payday is another two weeks away. You haven't *really* prayed until the doctor has told you they found a spot or a lump, and they don't know what it is or how to treat it. You haven't *really* prayed until you've had some *real* problems.

God may be using your problems to improve your prayer life. When you face a dilemma, don't distance yourself from God — deepen your devotion. Don't stop praying in your hurt or your angst — start praying more. Don't stop getting in the word because you don't know what to do next — start getting in the word even heavier. When you're struggling with where or how or when to go, go directly to God.

This was not the first time Hezekiah had found himself faced with difficult odds. It was not the first time he had received some bad news. Remember it was in the previous chapter that he found himself facing a threat from a powerful enemy, and letters were sent to him that he took and spread out in the house of the Lord. (2 Kings 19:14)

He took the evil report before God, and God stepped in, and He turned it around. He rerouted the Assyrian army and saved the lives of the Hezekiah and the people of Judah.

So, Hezekiah had a history of going to God and seeing Him turn things around in Hezekiah's favor. Hezekiah had a history of God performing miracles; he had what we might call a "faith file." You don't want to forget about how faithful God has been in the past because what He's done in the past is an indication of what you can expect Him to do in the present. When you remember what God has done, it will remind you of what God will do; and if He did it before, He can do it again.

He Reached Out for Deliverance from God

We all need to keep a faith file, like an up-to-date credit report on God. Credit reports are essential today because, ultimately, they are a reflection of one's character. A person's credit report tells you whether they are reliable or dependable, and it generally tells you whether you can trust them or not. God's credit report proves He's credible. It shows He's reliable, honest, true to His word, trustworthy, dependable, consistent, and faithful. You have to keep a record of all the things God has done for you in the past, including all He's brought you out of, all He's brought you through, all He's brought you over, and all He's brought you from under. You need an accurate list of past things God has done in your life, a file you've saved for each year, and at each stage of what you trusted God with or for, whether it was for you or someone close to you. The record may say:

He provided my college tuition in 2003!

He blessed me to graduate on a wing and a prayer in 2005!

He healed my mother in 2010!

He blessed me to survive a car wreck in 2011!

He brought my child through her surgery when she had her spleen removed in 2012!

He kept my wife when the wheels on her car could've caused her to go over an embankment in 2014!

You need to remember what God has done in the past to remind you of what He will do in the present. Remember all the tears He's dried up, all the mountains He's leveled, and the valleys He's exalted. Remember the battles He's fought, the enemies He's diverted, and the victories He's won.

Hezekiah may have been told in the past that it was pointless to pray. He may have been told at one time that his faith was futile. He may have been told before that he wasn't going to make it out. But God had turned things around for Hezekiah too many times, and if He did it before, surely He can do it again. If he protected, provided, preserved, and proved himself to be faithful in the past, He will do it again in the present. You can't make me doubt Him — I know too much about Him! If He did it before, in Jesus' Name, He can do it again!

Notice that Hezekiah negotiates based on his faithfulness to God. He recites his record of righteousness. You need to build some equity in your relationship with God, as He can hear you better when you have been faithful in following Him. There is a reward for righteous living. Serving the Lord will not just give you a future in Heaven, but favor on earth. That's one of the benefits of a relationship: if you live a life that honors God, God will honor you and honor your prayers. *"The effectual fervent prayer of the righteous avails much!"* (James 5:16)

Notice how Hezekiah prays. He prays a fervent and effectual prayer. He prayed from his heart, sincerely, strongly, and precisely.

He prays *sincerely*, with no pretense or special words.

He prays *strongly*, weeping bitterly and crying out to God from his soul. He prays *precisely*, stating that he wants to live and not die.

God responds to passionate pleas. See, real prayer involves you making some noise and showing some passion. Hannah went to the house of worship, and scripture says she poured out her soul. She cried, and she pleaded with everything in her, and God blessed her with a child.

Check out what Hezekiah does. He gets down, and he prays and pleads his case. I like this because Hezekiah did not just lay down and accept the report he was given. Listen, you don't just have to lay there and accept defeat, depression, or sickness. Regardless of what comes your way, you've got to pray until something happens!

You have to show God that you are not willing to accept some things in your life. In Luke 18, Jesus gave the parable of a woman who was persistent with her issue, who even stalked the judge (she camped out at the courthouse!), asking him to overturn a verdict or change a situation. Ultimately, scripture says, her persistence paid off, and the judge granted her request. That's how we must pray. We must pray with some perseverance and refuse to accept certain things as the final verdict. Consider, what could we change if we just weren't willing to accept it? In some instances, we have to remember God's promises and reject anything contrary as a temporary situation. Hezekiah gives us an example when he decided he was not going to die. He did not willingly receive the prophet's message but cried out to God on his own behalf.

CHAPTER 9

The Reversal for Hezekiah

God Changed His Condition And His Conclusion

God stopped the prophet Isaiah after he left Hezekiah's palace and told him to turn around. God told him to tell Hezekiah that He had heard his prayers and had seen his tears. God said to go back and tell Hezekiah that his life was going to be extended. Isaiah turned back around with a different word for the king. His first message was that Hezekiah would die and not live. But he went back to report that Hezekiah would live and not die.

God has the power and reserves the right to reverse your situation. Have you ever had God change conditions for you? Have you had God clear up your credit report or your status with the IRS? Maybe you had a medical visit where they saw a spot somewhere, but it was no longer there on the follow-up visit. Perhaps they said you owed, but somehow there is no longer a balance on the records. Have you ever had a word reversed in your life? Have you ever had God update your status? Isaiah turned around and told Hezekiah that he would live! He instructed Hezekiah to put some figs on the sore. At that time, figs were used for medical purposes. They would make an ointment from the figs, and the servants spread it on the sore area. We see that Hezekiah's healing comes by way of both miracle and medicine. You must realize that God can heal you by medical means or miraculous means. He can heal through surgery or the supernatural. If you are sick, don't resist treatment; obey the doctors' orders because the doctors' orders may be how God miraculously changes your malady.

Hezekiah's healing took some time, it was not immediate, but gradually he became well. He had to go through treatment. He got the word from God that he would recover, but his turnaround took a little time. God will turn your situation around, but the reality is sometimes it will not happen right away. God gave Hezekiah fifteen more years of life. He would be living on borrowed time. Actually, all of us are. We all have been given, by God, a specific allotted amount of time on this earth. That means we should live it wisely, not as fools. As Moses prayed, *"So teach us to number our days, that we may apply our hearts unto wisdom."* (Psalm 90:12)

Hezekiah told Isaiah that he wanted a sign from God that he was healed. He wanted to see proof of the miracle. In response, God does something unusual, uncommon, and unheard of. He turned back the hands of time. This is the first mention of any means of marking time.

In Hezekiah's day, Egyptian sundials were sometimes made in the form of miniature staircases, and the shadow moved up and down the stairs as time progressed. At Hezekiah's request, the shadow on the plate of the sundial called The Stairway of Ahaz reversed, or went backward, by ten degrees. How was this possible? Was the earth's rotation halted? Astronomers have determined that there was an eclipse of the sun during this time, near 701 BC. (3) This is considered the very first mention of daylight saving time. This was a phenomenon that defied science, as God turned the sun around. God demonstrates his omnipotence and his omniscience, showcasing His complete control over the fields of science, medicine, history, time, and nature. Our prayers have the power to move heaven and earth and make miracles happen. God shows us our prayers can alter any situation and turn it around.

This wasn't the only time God altered the natural order of things to do the supernatural for somebody. I believe that when He deems it necessary, God will change the natural order of things to do something supernatural in your situation.

Lazarus lay dead in the tomb for three days. They told Jesus He was too late. But He showed up and turned it around.

Several years after Sarah had passed childbearing age, she laughed when told she would have a baby. She said it was too late. But God turned it around.

Three days after they hung Him high and stretched Him wide, three days after He hung His head and died for you and me, He got up out of the grave. God turned it around.

There is no situation that God cannot turn around. Hezekiah's sickness was designed to show that no matter how seemingly irreversible a situation seems, God can still turn it around. I suggest to you that the illness was a setup and that the malady was designed for the making of a miracle. He can fix it. He can change it. Not only *can* He do it, but He *will* do it. Your current condition won't be your conclusion. Be not dismayed; whatever happens, God will take care of you. God will turn it around!

Section 4:

Get Ready for Rain

1 Kings 18:41-46

41 Then Elijah said to Ahab, "Go up, eat and drink; for there is the sound of abundance of rain."

42 So Ahab went up to eat and drink. And Elijah went up to the top of Carmel; then he bowed down on the ground, and put his face between his knees,

43 and said to his servant, "Go up now, look toward the sea." So he went up and looked, and said, "There is nothing." And seven times he said, "Go again."

44 Then it came to pass the seventh time, that he said, "There is a cloud, as small as a man's hand, rising out of the sea!" So he said, "Go up, say to Ahab, Prepare your chariot, and go down before the rain stops you."

45 Now it happened in the meantime that the sky became black with clouds and wind, and there was a heavy rain. So Ahab rode away and went to Jezreel.

46 Then the hand of the Lord came upon Elijah; and he girded up his loins and ran ahead of Ahab to the entrance of Jezreel.

For those of us who are urbanites and city dwellers, rain is a bit of a nuisance. We don't like storms or rain or even cloudy days. But for people who live in rural areas – farmers, in particular – rain, is not a nuisance; it is a necessity. In the ancient Jewish culture and the Middle East, the rain was akin to their greatest commodities. Because the people were agricultural, clouds and rain did not indicate a time of sadness but brought about a time of celebration. Rain was a symbol of God's favor, a sign of prosperity, and something people looked forward to having. Rain was essential to Israel's economy; it was the people's source of survival. It was necessary for their livestock, for their plants and vegetation, for the crops, and the ground. Without rain, their economy came to a screeching halt, and the situation became dire and dismal.

That's where the nation of Israel finds itself at this moment. They are dealing with a severe drought, a dry season with seemingly no end in sight. Israel has been unfaithful to God and involved in idolatry; because of this, God has shut up the heavens and refused to release the rain.

When things were going well, the people attributed their success to Baal and credited him for bringing the rainfall that allowed them to be prosperous and productive. So, God tells the prophet, Elijah, to go and tell Israel they got this thing mixed up and got God Himself messed up! He instructs

Elijah to go and tell Ahab that He alone is the One who makes it rain. To prove it, God withheld rain until an appointed time.

There was no rain, dew, and moisture in the land for three and a half years. Riverbeds dried up, brooks became barren, ponds were nothing more than scorched earth. For three and a half years, livestock perished, produce was non-existent, and the land was stricken with disease, deprivation, and starvation as this drought wore on and on. Then God does something absolutely astonishing. He entrusts the prophet Elijah with the word that it is soon going to rain. This word was for Elijah, but it's the word God has given me to share with you as we look at the life of this mighty man of God.

CHAPTER 10

Elijah Perceived that it would Rain

He Sensed It

Amidst the devastation and crippled economy, God entrusted Elijah with a message of hope and expectation that He was getting ready to send rain. This message would have seemed a bit strange during this crisis, and it would have been a bit of a struggle for the prophet to deliver. Here it is, the middle of a three-year drought, and Elijah is saying it's going to rain. People would have thought he was off and that he was incorrect in his prediction. They would have questioned his prophetic integrity and accuracy. But, God said get ready for rain. Elijah gives a weather forecast for rain in the middle of the worst and longest drought in Israel. Like a modern meteorologist, Elijah predicts the forecast, but he does so without modern technology. At God's direction, he shares with Ahab that he senses it's going to rain.

Through doppler radar, modern meteorologists have the ability to detect and perceive rainfall. Their radars reveal when rain, snow, or hailstorms will take place. They can perceive things in the heavenly realm which enables them to make certain predictions. If they say there will be an ice storm, we start buying up food, salt, shovels, and things because we trust their prediction.

In the same way, God's spirit allows our spirit man to pick up on things, to hear and see things and perceive things in the heavenly realm. The Holy Spirit gives us the ability to pick up things the natural man cannot perceive.

Elijah had an inner ear, a spiritual sixth sense, he didn't *see* the rain, but he *sensed* the rain. Our five senses give us access to the earthly realm. Our seeing, hearing, tasting, smelling, and feeling allow us to experience the world around us and help us to interpret what we need to make wise choices for ourselves and others. The Holy Spirit is like a sixth sense. He allows us to sense and understand things in the spirit realm in addition to the earth realm. He allows us to see things using more than our natural senses. *"Eye has not seen, nor ear heard, nor have entered into the heart of man the things which God has prepared for those who love Him. But God has revealed them to us through His Spirit"* (1 Corinthians 2:9-10). Those who operate only in the natural realm can neither see nor comprehend what those in the spirit realm can see and sense (1 Corinthians 2:14). The Holy Spirit gives us our spiritual sixth sense. He allows us to see what others cannot see and makes us aware of things others are not aware of. Because we have God's Spirit and faith in God, we don't look at the things that are seen but the things that are not seen. Furthermore, we walk by faith and not by sight, faith that has eyes and faith that has ears. Our faith can hear and see things in the spirit realm that others cannot.

When we learn to use our spiritual sixth sense and operate by faith, it will cause us to sense things that don't seem to make sense in the natural but make sense to us spiritually. We aren't just interpreting things in the natural sense, like what we see or hear, but we operate more heavily upon our sixth sense of faith. It was Elijah's spiritual sense that perceived it would rain.

When the great tsunami took 250,000 lives, there were stories about how many of the animals, particularly elephants, could sense the tsunami before it showed up. They sensed it, and in response, they took off to higher ground. See, God allows us to be able to sense things that others cannot. When we are connected to God, He enhances our spiritual senses to perceive things natural-minded people cannot. Discernment is not just being able to read people, but moments, seasons, and situations.

He Spoke It

Elijah heard the sound of rain pouring in his soul. He said it would rain before he ever saw the rain. It was so strong in his spirit that he spoke it to the king. In verse 41, he said, "There is the sound of abundance of rain." Notice the message is only for King Ahab at this time; it's not for everybody to hear just yet. Everybody was not yet ready to receive it.

Everybody reading this is not ready to receive the message just yet, but I hear the sound of rain! I hear God saying that He's getting ready to change the climate and conditions for anyone unemployed or underemployed, for anyone experiencing a dry spell or a drought season, for anyone whose business has been struggling, and for those who have had to take a pay cut and have been looking for a breakthrough. I hear the sound of an abundance of rain!

Elijah decreed and declared what the Lord had revealed. He began to speak those things which were not as though they were (Romans 4:17). He began to speak about things that had not yet happened. He didn't just discern it; he decreed it! Elijah sensed it was going to rain, and by faith, he started saying it would rain. Elijah could not only sense it was going to rain, but he also had the authority to say it was going to rain.

God won't just give you the ability to sense certain things, but He will give you the authority to say certain things as well. He wants you to have the power to speak His revealed word over yourself and your situation.

When you are sick, say, "I'm well!"

When you are weak, say, "I'm strong!"

When you are poor, say, "I'm rich!"

When you are in debt, say, "I'm free!"

When you are unemployed, say, "I'm transitioning to better!"

When you feel like you are at the bottom, say, "I'm the head and not the tail!"

When you are in a financial drought, say, "I hear the sound of rain!"

Your words are so powerful. Proverbs 18:21 says, "*Death and life are in the power of the tongue.*" In 1 Corinthians 4:13, Paul said, "*We also believe and therefore speak.*" In other words, our faith doesn't just give us the ability to sense certain things, but it provides us with authority to say certain things. That's why you have to learn to speak God's word over your life. When you speak God's word, you are releasing your faith into the atmosphere.

If God has put something in your spirit that you're expecting Him to do, you have to begin to decree and declare it. You have to decree and declare that doors are going to open for you. Decree and declare that you're going to build some kingdom connections this year. Decree and declare that you're going to be healthier and more fit. Decree and declare that you're going to do things this year that you would never have thought were possible. Decree and declare that God is getting ready to give you provision for your vision. Sense it and say it!

Speak into the atmosphere, "I can have what I decree! I believe it belongs to me, so I'm going to speak into the atmosphere!" Speak life over your home, speak life over your job, speak life over *yourself*. You don't just have the ability to sense what God is about to do, but you have the authority to say what God is going to do! Amen!!

CHAPTER 11

Elijah Prayed that it would Rain

He Has A Posture Of Prayer

Elijah puts himself in a posture of prayer, down on the ground with his head in between his knees (verse 42). After he gets the promise of rain from God, he goes and prays for rain. While he received God's word that it would rain, Elijah still realized that he needed to pray for God's word to come forth; and that is a lesson for you and me. Even when you've got a promise from God, you still need to pray until what God promised you comes forth.

Notice that Elijah's head is between his knees. He's praying and pushing, pregnant with a promise that requires prayer to push it out. God can give you a promise and cause you to see something happening, but you still need to pray. Even when it's all looking up and things look promising, when it appears everything is lining up, and it seems like what God has for you is coming together, you need to learn to pray until it happens.

Prayer is your part in the birthing process. It's the process of pushing out the promises of God in your life. Just like an expectant mother in the delivery room, who still has to put forth an effort to bring out her promise, so must we pray to see God's promises manifested in our lives. We must learn to pray until something happens.

Prayer is an exercise designed to build your faith. James 5:15-16 says we are to pray the prayer of faith to be raised up by the Lord and that the effectual fervent prayers of the righteous avail much. In that same chapter, James discusses the prayers of Elijah. This example of Elijah praying for rain is an example of a prayer of faith. Faith shouldn't cause you not to pray; faith should cause you to pray, even more fervently and intensely. In fact, praying helps you to believe God for what you have been praying about. How do you know that what you are asking for will come to pass? Because you've been praying about it! How do you know the business is going to get off the ground? Because you've been praying about it! How do you know your health will improve? Because you've been praying about it! How do you know your child's behavior is going to improve? Because you've been praying about it! I believe because I've been praying, and because I've been praying, I believe.

Remember: If God is going to perform what He promised in your life, you MUST pray!

Notice in the text that Elijah is praying, but nothing is happening. God promised him rain, but he still didn't see any rain. The servant is sent out to look for something, but he says there is nothing. It didn't look like anything was happening, but Elijah kept on pushing. He kept on praying until something started to happen, and soon it did.

George Muller was the founder of a large orphanage in Bristol, England. There were 300 children he cared for, and the house mother informed them there was no food. He had the children gather around the table in the dining area and told them to pray, giving thanks for the food they were going to receive. The children bowed their heads in prayer, and just as they finished, there was a knock at the door. The baker down the street brought them enough fresh bread to feed them all. In the same instance, a milkman's cart broke down outside of the orphanage, and by the time the repair would be complete, the milk would spoil, so they received all of the fresh milk. Within minutes after their prayer, God gave them the provisions, but they couldn't see that something was happening while they were praying. (4)

Don't ever think nothing is happening when you pray. Something is always happening in response to your prayer. Somebody reading this is just like Elijah's servant. You have been praying and looking for a sign of something favorable, something good happening, but you haven't seen anything. You've polished up your resume, you've searched, you've made calls, and gone on interviews, but it doesn't look like anything has opened up. You're getting a little discouraged and frustrated because you've done everything you know to do. You've prayed, you've obeyed God and put forth the effort to get the desired result, but you see nothing. I want to remind you to keep going after the thing God gave you to go after. Your persistence will pay off!

His Persistence Paid Off

Elijah sent his servant to check for rain, and on the seventh time, he saw a small cloud that looked like a man's hand. For a while, it didn't look like anything was happening, but something was, in fact, happening. As true as it was for Elijah, it is so for you. That's why you have to keep walking by faith, moving by faith, and looking for that thing God spoke in your spirit.

God says, "Go! Look again!" He is telling you to go back to that same place you sent your resume, go back to that same place that turned you down, follow-up on that lead, meet with that person again, revisit that idea, give them another call, try that thing again, give it another shot. In Matthew 7:7, Jesus said to ask, seek, and knock—keep on until you get what you're looking for. Keep asking until you get it, keep seeking until you find it, keep knocking until the door opens up. Persistence pays off.

You might be thinking to yourself, *"But, that's too much!"* You may be concerned about seeming strange or looking desperate, being perceived as though you are sweating those people, or just coming across like a fool. That's pride talking. See, sometimes our pride will cause us to miss out on blessings because we're so worried about our image. Can you imagine what Elijah's servant thought and how frustrated he was? Here it was that Elijah told him to look again time after time after time—seven times total. He kept going up and down the mountain to the sea and coming back, saying there's nothing. I applaud this servant because each time Elijah said "Go," he didn't complain. He just did what he was asked without worrying how he might look. When you're looking for rain, you have to be willing to look strange. When you're pursuing the promises of God, you have to be willing to look odd. When you're going after something God has said and shown you, you might look like a crazy gold prospector, like you may be on a wild goose chase or foolish mission, but that idea cannot stop you from going.

Consider the story of Noah in Genesis chapters 6-8. He must have looked insane, expecting it to rain. It took years before what God revealed to him was realized; but, when it rained,

Noah stood up in his God-given blessing as everyone else realized he was right all along.

Sometimes what you're looking for will take time and will involve multiple efforts and diligence before you get it. Faith says that even when it doesn't happen the first time, you don't stop, but you keep showing up until you see it. His servant came back after the seventh time and reported that he had seen something. A cloud in the sky that's the size of a hand might seem trivial or inconsequential, but Elijah knew that while the cloud was small, it was significant. That cloud carried the content of what he had been expecting. That cloud carried what it was that they wanted. Like Elijah, you have to realize the potential in the small things. Everything big started small; everything significant started insignificantly.

Maybe you got a call from a company to come in for an interview, and they offered you an entry-level position. It's a small cloud; keep looking for rain.

Maybe you took out a small loan to start your business, and it is still not turning a large profit. It's a small cloud; keep looking for rain.

Maybe your child is not on the honor roll yet, but he is not misbehaving in class like last year. It's a small cloud; keep looking for rain.

Maybe you don't have a commercial kitchen and had to start selling dinners out of your car, showing up to barber shops, beauty salons, and pop-up shops in the interim. It's a small cloud; keep looking for rain.

Maybe you can't afford a garage right now, but you have a small operation working on cars in your driveway. It's a small cloud; keep looking for rain.

Maybe the sanctuary holds just a little over 200 people right now, and the parking lot is kind of small. Maybe we have plans to expand the sanctuary and the parking lot and even open a second daycare center. It's a small cloud right now, but we keep looking for rain.

When God puts something in your spirit, it may start small; but don't despise the day of small things. *Keep looking for rain.*

CHAPTER 12

Elijah Prepared for the Rain

Get Ready...Its going To Rain

Elijah told Ahab to prepare his chariot because God was about to send the rain. In fact, he said God is about to send so much rain that he would not be ready for it, and it may stop him in his tracks. When Elijah warned Ahab, it was still dry with barely a cloud in the sky; it didn't look like there could be nor would be any rain. But Elijah said it's going to rain, so get ready.

You may be experiencing a dry spell or a dry season. You may only see barrenness around you, but God says to get ready for rain! Get ready for that change in the climate you've been praying for. Get ready for the interview! Get ready for the promotion! Get ready for the raise! Get ready for the new position! Get ready for the career change! Get ready for the influx of new customers! New business ideas are coming! New employment opportunities are coming! Despite what it may look like, favor and approval are coming down like rain! Resources from multiple streams are coming down like rain! Doors that were previously shut are opening! Get ready — it's going to rain!

Get ready! God is going to send something that you won't see coming. It will catch you off guard and may surprise you. Get ready — the phone call is coming that could change your life. Get ready — the deal of a lifetime is just around the corner. Get ready — that hard-to-move property is going to sell. Get ready — windfall profits and returns on investment are coming your way. You may not see it, but God is working in response to your prayers. Get ready for rain!

I once read about a drought in a town in Oklahoma when the church called everyone together for a special prayer meeting to ask God to send rain. They came in droves to the church to gather for this prayer session. One of the members, an older lady, showed up with an umbrella, and they looked at her strangely because it had not rained for so long. Finally, someone asked her why she had an umbrella when it wasn't raining. She responded, "I thought we were coming to pray for rain, so I came prepared for the rain."

Elijah began to move like it was going to rain. He hadn't seen the rain, but he heard about that small cloud, and he jumped up and started moving quickly. He hadn't seen the first raindrop, but he ran in advance and started warning people to get in position for the rain.

Don't only come to God praying for Him to bless you, but, in conjunction with your prayers, go on and prepare for God to bless you. God is going to give you an expectant blessing. I heard there's rain in the forecast. I believe God is going to do something you've been expecting Him to do for a while. Are you prepared? There's going to be a great outpouring of God's favor in your life. Are you ready to receive it? Your drought is about to end, and the outpouring may stop you in your tracks if you're not in position. Claim His promise for your life. God will do exceedingly, abundantly, above all that you're asking (Ephesians 3:20).

Some Native American tribes had a ceremonial ritual that they referred to as the rain dance. They would perform or dance and sing to invoke rain and to ensure the protection of the harvest. They would take this very seriously, dressing in fancy apparel, adding elaborate feather headdresses, and decorating their bodies with bold colors. They would stomp their feet on the ground as if to make the sound of falling rain, and they would open their mouths and look up in anticipation for the rain to fall.

I believe we can learn something from this practice in many Native American communities. We need to learn how to pray and prepare for rain by looking up to Heaven, lifting up our voices, stomping our feet, and dancing to the beat. We should look up to heaven, open our mouths, and begin to dance in anticipation of the rain God is sending. I lift my hands because I believe it's getting ready to rain. I lift my voice because it's getting ready to rain. I move my feet because it's getting ready to rain.

Section 5:

Prayer is Still the

Answer

James 5:13-18

13 Is anyone among you suffering? Let him pray. Is anyone cheerful? Let him sing psalms.

14 Is anyone among you sick? Let him call for the elders of the church, and let them pray over him, anointing him with oil in the name of the Lord.

15 And the prayer of faith will save the sick, and the Lord will raise him up. And if he has committed sins, he will be forgiven.

16 Confess your trespasses to one another, and pray for one another, that you may be healed. The effective, fervent prayer of a righteous man avails much.

17 Elijah was a man with a nature like ours, and he prayed earnestly that it would not rain; and it did not rain on the land for three years and six months.

18 And he prayed again, and the heaven gave rain, and the earth produced its fruit.

I believe the most powerful thing we have available on earth is prayer. Pastor Adrian Rogers once wrote that "Prayer is our greatest Christian privilege and our greatest Christian failure." (9) Prayer is a Christian's greatest power, yet I believe prayer may be one of the most neglected areas of our Christian lives.

Some question the validity and value of prayer. Some of us wonder if our praying really makes a difference or if God even hears us when we pray. It is of vital importance that children of God understand and appreciate the power and potency of prayer.

James, the brother of Jesus, shares with us both the validity of prayer and the value of prayer. In six short verses, he mentions prayer seven times. When something is repeated in the Bible, it's repeated for a reason—so we can recognize its importance in God's message. What God, through James, wants us to recognize is the power of prayer.

CHAPTER 13

Exhortation to Pray

Prayer Is Advised For Every Ailment

To "exhort" means to urge, strongly encourage, to give advice as an urgent appeal. James exhorts us to pray in response to any and every problem we have. He says whenever you are suffering, pray; whenever you are sick, pray; and whenever you are in sin, pray. Prayer is the prescription regardless of the circumstance. Whether the issue is physical, emotional, psychological, or spiritual, prayer can fix it. Prayer is designed to treat every ache and every pain, as well as any difficulty, any disturbance, or any discomfort.

My mother grew up in a family with ten siblings, and they didn't have a lot of money to go to doctors for medicine. She told me they used aspirin for every ailment they had. She said it worked for every sting, throb, or sore they had; they reached for aspirin when they had a toothache, headache, backache, every-ache because it was an answer for just about everything.

That's what we must understand about prayer. Prayer is still the best answer for every ailment, the solution for every situation, and is sufficient for every form of suffering. We must learn to pray for every problem we face, and prayer should be our first response, not our last resort.

It seems that we have moved away from prayer, even in the church. We seem to look outside of what God prescribed to solve our problems. We look to psychiatrists, medication, therapists, and other professional counselors to address the issues that arise in our lives. Certainly, all of these things can and should be used, and all of these treatments have their place; but none of these things should take the place of prayer. Take your prescription and pray. Spend time with a therapist and spend time with God.

We must be practical, but we also must pray. I'm very practical, and the Bible is very practical. The book of James is perhaps the most practical in the New Testament. But, as practical as the Bible or I may be, I still believe the best prescription for any problem is prayer. Prayer can heal you when the doctors can't. Prayer can pay the bill when you don't have money. Prayer can persuade the judge and the jury when the lawyer can't. Prayer can fix the problem on your job when HR can't. Prayer can give you a better deal than your negotiating skills can. Prayer is still the answer!

It is absolutely appropriate to utilize counseling, medicine, and treatments for mental, emotional, and even physical issues. Still, the first and the best thing I can prescribe to you is prayer. Prayer should be your first line of offense, not your last line of defense. It's the real remedy you should reach for. Before you go to the doctor's office, you ought to pray. Before you put the child on Ritalin, you ought to pray. Before you get a divorce lawyer, pray. Before you seek counseling, pray. If you decide to get counseling, still pray. If you take the medication, still pray. If you get legal advice, still pray. Prayer is still the answer.

There should be some blessed oil in your medicine cabinet next to the Band-Aids, the Tylenol, and the Vicks VapoRub. When your child is not doing well in school, when you are sick in your body, when you and your spouse are at odds, and when there is turmoil and confusion in your life, you should take out that oil and anoint that entire situation. Lay hands on your child's bed, anoint your bedroom, anoint the doorposts of your home, and even lay hands on yourself. Prayer. Still. Works.

Prayer Is An Antidote To Anxiety

So often, the problem is that we tend to *overthink* and *under* pray. As a result, we find ourselves filled with anxiety and falling into a panicked state. Scripture says, *"Be anxious for nothing, but in everything by prayer and supplication, with thanksgiving let your requests be made known to God; and the peace of God will guard your heart and mind."* (Philippians 4:6-7)

Sometimes we have the mindset that we need God for the big things and think we are bothering God by discussing smaller things in our lives. But, think about this: Can you think of anything that might happen in our lives that God would consider "big??" Everything we deal with is small to Him! So, don't just bring to Him what you think is big enough for Him; bring Him *everything*.

If the issue is big enough to bother you, it's big enough to bring to God in prayer!

Anything that gives you mental or emotional anguish you are to bring to God. It's often the little things you face that mess with you the most. It's those so-called little things that gnaw at you and drain you and keep you up at night, threatening your rest and peace at every turn. That's what God wants you to pray about.

There's a story told of a missionary who spent his first night out in the African Bush. He was so afraid of lions, and he prayed over and over, "God, please protect me from the lions!" He woke up the next day with these huge mosquito bites all over his body. He was miserable. One of the people in his company remarked, "You prayed for God to protect you from the big thing; you should have asked him to protect you from the small things."

The small things are the things you should pray about. Those are the things that get to you, gnaw at you, and can make you miserable.

Don't worry about anything, but pray about everything. That means we are to pray at all times about all things. When you pray at all times about all things, you will find yourself less anxious. When we go to God in prayer, we will enjoy God's peace.

Pray More...Worry Less! Some of us are paranoid about things because we don't pray about things. We talk to everybody but God, and often that advice leaves us more anxious, and that counsel leaves us more concerned. It's no wonder some of us are easily panicked—we won't pray! A praying person is a powerful person and is protected by God's promises. The effective, fervent prayers of the righteous avail much!

Prayer is like a powerful antibody to anxiety. Antibodies counter the bacteria that build up in your body and threaten to make you sick and keep you from functioning. God designed prayer as an antibiotic to help against your anxiety. The Doctor prescribes it, and the answers to some of your ailments you can only get through Him. Prayer is a means of both prevention and cure. Psychological studies have proven that people who pray are less likely to need counseling and are mentally healthier than those who do not pray. (10) Isaiah 26:3 reminds us that He will keep us in perfect peace if we keep our minds stayed on Him. Prayer brings healing to the ailments of mankind - mental, spiritual, physical, and emotional. James 5:13 says, *"If any among you is afflicted, let him pray."*

Dr. Alexis Carrel said, "As a physician, I have seen men after all other therapy had failed, lifted out of disease and melancholy by the serene effort of prayer." (2)

Regardless of the circumstances, prayer can take the pressure off and restore your peace. When you put your problems in God's hand, God will place His peace in your heart. It's one great gift exchange.

CHAPTER 14

The Effectiveness of Prayer

There Must Be Persistence

Never underestimate the power of prayer. Prayer is potent. Perhaps you've heard the saying, "No prayer, no power; more prayer, more power!" See, prayer not only affects you, but it also affects things around you. Prayer changes things. Notice James says that those who are sick will get well, and those in sin will be forgiven. Things happen when you pray.

Please don't think you are wasting time when you pray. Don't see it as an exercise of futility that does not produce results. One of the challenges to us praying is thinking that our prayers are in vain and that praying is not worth your time. But, don't stop praying! Pray without ceasing (1 Thessalonians 5:17). You have to ask, you have to seek, and you have to knock, but God will answer. (Matthew 7:7-8)

Sometimes it will seem like your prayers aren't working and effective, but keep praying. While you are praying, God is working. Don't stop praying, don't stop fasting, and don't stop pleading. God is answering.

This testimony is from the late George Muller:

In November 1844, I began to pray for the conversion of five individuals. I prayed every day without a single intermission, whether sick or in health, on the land, on the sea, and whatever the pressure of my engagements might be. Eighteen months elapsed before the first of the five was converted. I thanked God and prayed on for the others. Five years elapsed, and then the second was converted. I thanked God for the second and prayed on for the other three. Day by day, I continued to pray for them, and six years passed before the third was converted. I thanked God for the three and went on praying for the other two. These two remained unconverted.

Thirty-six years later, he wrote that the other two, sons of one of Muller's friends, were still not converted. He wrote, "but I hope in God, I pray on, and look for the answer. They are not converted yet, but they will be." In 1897, fifty-two years after he began to pray daily, without interruption, for these two men, they were finally converted — but after he died! Muller understood what Luke meant when he introduced a parable Jesus told about prayer, saying, "Then Jesus told His disciples a parable to show them that they should always pray and not give up..." Luke 18:1 (8)

Indeed, the prayers we lift to God even go beyond our lifetime.

In Luke 18, Jesus gives the parable of the persistent widow. The woman has a need and request to give to an evil man. This man had no mercy, and she had to plead with him. This man is an unjust judge with no character and no compassion but eventually grew so tired of her that he relented. She had a burden, and she bothered him until she got her breakthrough. She bothered her way into a blessing. So much more will our God, who loves us, respond to us when we bring our cares to Him.

Persistent prayers produce miracles! If you never request it, you don't give God the opportunity to respond. Try this hashtag: #StartAskingGodForMore. Keep praying until it feels like you are bothering God and annoying God. Your input will determine your outcome! You get what you pray for!

There Must Be Purity

Prayer absolutely works, but if prayer is going to work for you, there are some conditions. Notice the wording in verse 16. It's the person who is righteous or in right standing with God who can be effective in prayer. By this, we can surmise that not all prayer gets to God. To be heard by God, you have to be in good standing with God. Some people are quick to say that they pray and they talk about praying, but God may not even hear their prayers; they never make it past the roof because they are not in good standing with God:

"Behold, the Lord's hand is not shortened, That it cannot save; Nor His ear heavy, that it cannot hear. But your iniquities have separated you from your God; And your sins have hidden His face from you, So that He will not hear." (Isaiah 59:1-2)

"The Lord is far from the wicked, But He hears the prayer of the righteous." (Proverbs 15:29)

"If I regard iniquity in my heart, the Lord will not hear." (Psalm 66:18)

See, prayer is communicating with God, and He gives believers an open line to His throne room. But you can't communicate with God properly if your lifestyle is not in sync with His word, His will, and His ways. As a Christian, if you live in open, unconfessed, unrepentant sin, it's hard for God to hear you. You can talk and talk, but the signal is lost.

I was on the phone with someone the other day, and we were talking, but the call dropped. They called back and apologized, explaining that the area they were in caused the call to drop. The communication was broken because of where they were at that time, and when they left the area they were in, they called back and picked up the conversation. After they were situated in the right place, our connection was uninterrupted.

As a Christian, you have fellowship with God, and He hears your prayers and your petitions. But when you get out of the will of God, it's hard for Him to hear you. So, you have to be in the proper position for that connection to work. When you break fellowship, the fellowship has to be restored. When you get situated in the right place again, He will hear what you are trying to say.

There Must Be Passion

James says the person praying should have integrity and some intensity if prayer is going to work. For the prayers to avail much, they have to be fervent. Fervent means intense, vehement, or passionate.

Prayer should not be something we do casually but something we do fervently. There should be some emotion, some zeal, some concentration. There should be some focus and drive, some energy. People should feel our prayers. There should be some passion.

Charles Spurgeon once said he who pleads (to God) without fervency does not plead at all! (11) You cannot commune with God, who is a consuming fire, if there is no fire in your prayers. Your prayers should have fire, faith, and fervor. It's the authentic passion that moves God when you cry out and moan to the One you know can address your needs. In 1 Samuel 1, Hannah had passion when she went before God in prayer. She cried, she moaned, she repeated herself — she gave it all to God. That's the kind of prayer that is effective and changes things. The Bible provides us with several examples of God's regard for passionate prayer:

"The Lord said, 'I have indeed seen the misery of my people in Egypt. I have heard them crying out because of their slave drivers, and I am concerned about their suffering. So I have come down to rescue them.'" (Exodus 3:7-8)

"And the Angel of the Lord said to her: Behold, you are with child, And you shall bear a son. You shall call his name Ishmael, Because the Lord has heard your affliction." (Genesis 16:11)

"In her deep anguish, Hannah prayed to the Lord, weeping bitterly. And she made a vow, saying, 'Lord Almighty, if you will only look on your servant's misery and remember me.'" (1 Samuel 1:10-11)

"In my distress I cried to the Lord, and He heard me." (Psalms 120:1)

"I love the Lord because He has heard my voice and my supplications." (Psalm 116:1)

These passionate pleas are the kinds of prayers that work and change things, get God's attention and *work*. You should cry out to God over your issues and concerns. Don't sit back, nonchalant, uncaring, and uninterested; you have to go in and get serious, praying to the Lord for healing and a breakthrough. Cry to the Lord to save your child. Implore Him to touch your spouse. Beseech the Lord to reveal Himself to you like never before.

There is power in prayer! Repeat this phrase to yourself: *Prayer equals POWER!*

CHAPTER 15

The Example of Prayer

It's Still Powerful

James is one of the most powerful men of prayer in the Old Testament. He points back to the prophet Elijah who lived centuries before this epistle was written. James begins his discussion about Elijah with the fact that Elijah was an average man like us. He had weaknesses, struggles, bouts of depression, doubt, and fear, but he believed in the power of prayer.

Sometimes we think the people of the Bible were different from us, that they were made of something special. They were human beings just like we are, but many of them just believed and operated by faith. That's the point James is making about Elijah.

Elijah was moved to pray for revival. He prayed that people would turn back to God. His prayers moved heaven and earth, and his prayers changed the conditions of his nation.

His prayers shook kings and kingdoms, impacted the economy, and changed the environment. That's the kind of praying we need to do in our nation today. We need to *"Cry aloud and spare not."* (Isaiah 58:1) More than ever, we need to plead the blood over this entire nation with intercessors that are determined to stand in the gap on behalf of this country.

By Elijah's prayers, the rain stopped for three years; and by his prayers, the rain returned. Elijah turned the water off, and then he prayed to turn it on again. James points back, and then he points forward to tell us that prayer still works.

Realize that your prayers can change things around you. I am a living witness that the same God who moved Elijah to pray and shifted the atmosphere can change conditions in your home, your family, and your world. I dare you to begin to pray over whatever situation in your life that needs shifting *right now.*

Whatever the problem, prayer will fix it!

Whatever the circumstance, prayer will fix it!

Whatever the ailment, prayer will fix it!

Whatever the issue, prayer will fix it!

I dare you to try God at His word. Pray in the morning, pray in the midnight hour, pray when trouble arises! Prayer still works!

It's Still Potent

I got sick not long ago, and I had a bad headache. Too weak to get up and see the doctor or go to the store, I looked around my home for the Excedrin. I had prayed; God is a healer, whether by medicine or miracle. When I found the Excedrin and I looked at the bottle, the date printed on it had passed. It was expired. So, I concluded that it was no longer strong enough or potent enough to fix my ailment. My wife, Roxie, told me not to pay any attention to the expiration date because it's still powerful and strong enough to work. I hesitated and asked her if she was sure about that. She repeated that I should go ahead and take it. Sure enough, about thirty minutes later, my pain was gone. Despite me thinking it wouldn't, it worked. Despite me thinking it was expired and outdated, it did what I needed it to do.

I know we live in a modern world with all kinds of remedies and prescriptions and methods and means of treating the issues of life, so some of us think that prayer is outdated and antiquated. We are told it worked back in the day because people were primitive and lacked other resources, but we doubt it has the same power today. I just want to remind you that prayer still works. It still works for sickness. It still works for stress. It still works for your struggles — prayer still works. It's still potent and just as powerful as it was before. Jesus is the same yesterday, today, and forever

(Hebrews 13:8). He still answers prayers. He still performs miracles. He still heals. He still delivers. He still fixes. He still changes things. *Prayer. Still. Works!!*

Section 6:

God is Waiting on Your Call

Jeremiah 33:3

3 Call to Me, and I will answer you, and show you great and mighty things, which you do not know.

So often when we think about God, we imagine Him being far away, off into the distance out of view and out of sight. We think of the reach of the sun, moon, and stars, and we envision God being billions of miles off into space. But Psalm 145:18 reminds us, *"The Lord is near to all who call upon Him, To all who call upon Him in truth."*

In other words, God is not as far away as we might imagine, and in a real sense, He is closer than you might think.

In this verse, the prophet Jeremiah reminds us of the nearness of God. He says God is closer than we think; in fact, He's just a call away. Jeremiah shares with us the availability of God and how we can access God. He says if you really want to get in touch with God, all you have to do is give God a call.

This passage is literally an invitation from God for us to pray. God wants us to understand that He is not hard to find, nor is He hard to contact. Communicating doesn't have to be complicated, and all we have to do is give Him a call.

God even makes it personal. He indicates that He wants everyone to know how to get in touch with Him, then lists His number and makes it public. He tells us that if we contact Him, we won't be disappointed.

CHAPTER 16

A Personal Request

God Demonstrates His Interest In Us

God initiates the conversation in this verse and tells us to call Him some time. He looks forward to hearing from us. That tells us just how interested God is in having a conversation with us. It tells us that He's thinking about us enough to give us this solicitation to reach out to Him. Isn't it amazing that God invites us to talk to Him personally? It really should flatter us, as it did for David.

In Psalm 8:3-4, David, a shepherd boy, looked up at a starlit night and said, *"When I consider Your heavens, the work of Your fingers, The moon and the stars, which You have ordained, What is man that You are mindful of him, And the son of man that You visit him?"*

Who are we, Lord, that You are interested in us enough to issue an invitation to converse with you? How does it make you feel that, as great as God is, He still wants to hear from you? It's a privilege to be able to say that we have a direct line to God. Some people like to name-drop about the significant people they have in their phone or their set of contacts. Well, I have the God of the universe, who made heaven and earth, on speed dial. In fact, I just got off the line with Him this morning. He told me I had a future and hope. He told me I'm fearfully and wonderfully made. He said I have a purpose and a plan. Talk about a name drop!

You and I should be flattered that God looks forward to hearing from us. He tells us that He's interested in what we have to say, that our feelings matter to Him and that what we have to say is worth being heard. Some of us think God is too big and we're too small and that there are so many more important things for Him to deal with than the things that concern us. God is telling us that no matter how big or small it is, we can call Him. God is not just *willing* to hear from you; He *wants* to hear from you. He wants to hear what you have to say, what's on your mind, and what's in your heart. He genuinely wants you to come to talk to Him, to share your innermost desires. He wants to hear your thoughts and build a relationship with you.

Sometimes we just need somebody to talk to. We want to talk, and we don't necessarily need immediate answers or feedback; we just want an ear to hear our hearts. So, we call up family or friends with the idea that we can express ourselves without being judged or misunderstood. We might call those same individuals at different moments of our lives or to celebrate something good or to share frustrations or even to cry. Those to whom we can talk about anything in our lives usually become the closest persons to us. God knows that, so He tells us that's what He wants to be to us. He wants us to see in Him a friend we can call on any time, for any reason. God is here for you when you need to vent, when you need a shoulder to cry on, and when you need a confidante or a sounding board to express your deepest feelings. God wants to be the One you call before you call your brother, sister, mother, or buddy. He's interested in hearing whatever you have to say.

Some people pay psychologists, psychiatrists, and counselors just so their hearts can be heard. Some people even go as far as to call psychic hotlines to express their concerns and address their fears. But here is the God of the universe who made the mind and the mouth we have as well as the world we live in, and He is willing and waiting to listen.

God Desires Intimacy With Us

This invitation is not just about telling God your problems, but it's also a request to get to know Him personally. Some of us only pray when we need something, but the relationship is just as important.

I'm sure you have somebody who only calls you or reaches out to you when they need something. Sometimes they don't even realize they are doing it. When you see their number on your phone, you pause and let it ring a few times because you're wondering if you really want to talk to them. Knowing it's either that they're in trouble, or they're asking for something, and you don't even know if you want to talk to them right now.

That's how some of us pray. We only go to God when we run into a problem. We only see prayer as a Help Hotline or an Emergency Number, crying, "God, help, I'm in trouble! God, emergency! Something's wrong! God, I need a job, like yesterday!" I think we forget or fail to realize that God has feelings. Scripture says God laughs (Psalm 37:13, Proverbs 1:26); He gets angry (Numbers 11:1-2); He is even grieved at times (Genesis 6:6). God is a person; He has a personality, and He has feelings. God wants us to come to Him in prayer and just say, "God, I'm not asking for anything; it's not an emergency. Everything is ok. I just want to say thank You for being a good friend. I was just thinking about You. I just wanted to hear Your voice."

When you start praying like that, God will start responding better to your prayers. God will start doing things you didn't even ask for, and He'll begin working things out just because you all are close. He'll start hooking you up and helping you avoid certain trouble because you all are tight like that. The way to really get to know a person is by talking to them, and the only way we get to know God better is through continual conversations with Him. The more you talk to God, the more you'll get to know Him. That's how intimacy is developed and established.

God wants to build a real relationship with you. He doesn't want you to have *religion* but a *relationship*. Signs of a real relationship are when you can just be yourself and talk with Him about whatever. You don't have to be formal. You are free to just be you with God in prayer. You don't have to speak in King James language:

"O God, thouest who sitteth between the Cherubim! The Lord of host is thy name! We come before you as humbly as we know how. Bowing down before you in submission, we give reverence to your righteous and holy name!"

You don't have to do all that!

God is not impressed with our religiosity; He's trying to build a real relationship with us. Jesus told us in Matthew 6:5-9 not to pray to be seen and heard, using eloquent words that He called "vain repetitions," which sound good but don't mean much. God knows what you need. You don't have to be formal with God. You are free to express yourself to God in your own way. God doesn't want a formal relationship with you; He wants a personal relationship with you. Your prayers should have a relaxed and conversational tone; it shouldn't be stiff or ceremonial. You might talk proper and formal with people when you have a formal relationship with them, but God does not want that type of relationship with you. Don't force yourself to have that cold and distant relationship with God; seek to have a more comfortable, intimate closeness with the Lord, where you talk personally to Him and express yourself just the way you are.

See, some of us don't pray because we hear other people pray, and we think we are not as articulate as they are or don't know how to speak or articulate as they do. So, we don't pray at all, or we do the conference calls where we have other people pray to God for us while we sit silently or say very little. Don't do a three-way — call God direct. Jesus is on the mainline. You call Him up and tell Him what you want!

Don't be afraid to bumble and stumble over your words as you pray. Prayer takes practice, and practice makes perfect. The more you pray, the more you will perfect it, and your prayers will become more effective. Just resist the urge not to pray. *"Men always ought to pray and not lose heart."* (Luke 18:1) God is waiting on your call.

CHAPTER 17

A Promise to Respond

He Will Respond Personally

When you call Him, God says you won't get a recorded greeting or a beep for an answering machine. No, He will personally answer. God would not go through the trouble of telling you to call Him and not give you a direct line that goes straight to Him.

I grew up catching the bus downtown to the Indianapolis Black Expo. My friends and I competed on who could get the most girls' telephone numbers. We would get home and call some of the numbers we had gotten and discover some of the numbers were bogus. The girls would have you convinced that they wanted you to call. Some girls would play you really good, talking about, "Here are two numbers! Okay, did you get it? Make sure you call! If I don't hear from you, I'll be mad!" But when we dialed 876-7676, the number would not connect us to them at all.

That's not God. He says He wants us to call Him, and that's what He means. He won't have you make an effort to contact Him and not respond or leave you hanging. He's not like that; the Lord is genuinely interested in you and is waiting on your call.

I grew up with two sisters, and sometimes they would give boys their phone number, and when the boys would call, they would refuse to answer. They would call and say, "Is Diana there?" and it was my job to find out who it was, say his name out loud, and my sister would signal me to tell him she wasn't there. I would say into the phone, "Man, she said she's not here!" (Yes, I was that brother! LOL!) Now that we have Caller ID, it helps us screen our calls to choose who to answer. Back then, though, I would ask my sisters why they would give the boy the number and then not answer? You made them think they really had a chance when in truth, you were not interested, and that's worse than not giving the number at all.

Thank God, He will talk with you any time. Whenever you call, He will conduct a conversation. When you pray, He will answer, and you and He will speak. Here's what we must remember about prayer: Prayer is not just a monologue where you do all the talking; prayer is dialogue, where you speak and allow God to speak back to you. A conversation is more than just you talking *to* someone; it's you talking *with* someone where you both bring something to the discussion.

Some of us are like folks who over-talk other people and don't allow them to respond. Talking with those types, no one can get a word in edgewise because they do all of the talking. That's rude, and it's a bad habit to talk to someone, and you do all the talking or strike up a conversation with someone and then don't allow them to contribute. A conversation is not only you talking, but it's also you listening. We think prayer is coming to God, and we do all the talking. Then, we get frustrated, and we run out of things to say. We say, "Okay, there, I've said everything, and I'm done." But prayer is not just you doing all the talking. It's also you taking time to let God express Himself and to respond to you. Prayer is not talking *at* God; it's talking *with* God, allowing Him to speak to your spirit. This is why we must learn to be still and listen to God. We need to understand the importance of silence and stillness. We need to learn to wait and meditate in prayer. It's a best practice to read your word before you pray, then bring your Bible, pen, and a notebook with you in prayer, expecting God to speak to you while you are waiting and still. Give God a chance to respond.

Sometimes we run to God's door, knock on it, and then run away (in other words, we end the prayer moment) before He can answer. We can initiate a quick prayer, telling God that we don't know what to do, need His help for this-or-that, then run off without waiting on God. Give God a chance to answer the door.

It Will Require Patience

You have to give God a chance to respond. That's why it is so important to set aside opportunities for quality time with God. It's going to take more than five minutes to pray. You need to create occasions to hear the Lord speaking. Turn off the cell phone and the television, shut down the computer, close the door, and protect your time with God. Anything else on your schedule can wait; you're talking with God. This takes time.

God will answer in His own time. Notice, He says He will answer, but He doesn't give us specifics. God says He will respond, but He doesn't give us a time frame. He's a God you can't hurry: He'll be there, don't you worry. He may not come when you want Him, but He's on time, every time. He answers according to His schedule. When you are in prayer and a conversation with God, you must remember that He is in control of all creation, and *He is in control of the conversation*. Let God take the lead. I'm convinced that God wants us to know He's in control and for us to just be still and know that He is God:

He moves when He gets ready. He speaks when He gets ready. He replies when He gets ready, and sometimes we've got to sit before the Lord and wait. It doesn't always take an hour, but sometimes it will. Other times it may even take longer. Our task is to sit down and camp out in the prayer closet, humble ourselves, and know He's God and He is worth waiting for.

We have to develop the discipline of prayer, and that discipline involves *patience*.

Prayer is allowing God to download His thoughts to us and speak to our souls. God is trying to download some information into our system, but we have to sit still and wait out the process. I've discovered that large files that carry a lot of content sometimes can take a while to be downloaded. At times God is trying to transfer data into your spirit that is so heavy it takes time. Prayer requires patience.

Several years ago, I was on the phone with the alarm company. I'd had several break-ins, and my alarm wasn't activated, so I called, and they had me on hold to speak to a customer service representative. I waited on hold for about fifteen minutes. It seemed like a waste of time, and I wasn't getting anywhere, but I knew I needed to talk to them so they could coach me through resetting my alarm system. Just as I decided that I was tired of waiting and chalked it up to a waste of time, I shifted to hang up the phone, and someone answered. Had I not been patient enough to wait, I would have missed the pertinent information I needed.

Sometimes we hang up or give up in prayer before we get an answer. Sometimes we miss what God has to say to us because we're not patient enough to sit until He's ready to speak. How many important things have we missed due to lack of patience? How many bad decisions have we made because of our unwillingness to wait on God's voice? How often have we moved forward without waiting and listening for God to advise us, coach us, and direct us on the path He has for us? Answered prayer involves patience and persistence—that is, knocking, seeking, and asking until we get an answer. You have to get down on our knees and not get up until we get through. You have to keep praying until God answers. Keep praying until you get your breakthrough. God is a rewarder of those who *diligently* seek Him.

CHAPTER 18

A Profound Reward

Access To Revelation

God says that He will show you great and mighty things you know not of. He will grant you exposure to things you didn't know existed. Unknown things. Unfathomable things. Unsearchable things. Things that the eye has not seen nor has the ear heard will be revealed to you in prayer (1 Corinthians 2:9).

I'm still amazed at the Internet. I'm awed at the amount of content you can reach at the push of a button. The information you can access in seconds is mind-boggling: historical facts, books, articles, quotes, stories, statistics, opportunities, people, marketplaces — there's just an untold wealth of knowledge. We stand in wonderment of the brilliance and genius of men like Steve Jobs and Bill Gates. But, consider this: Prayer is like a search engine. When you pray, you tap into the mind of the One who made the mind of even the most brilliant man. If God gave those who don't even profess Him the genius they possess, imagine what He wants to reveal to you in prayer.

See, prayer gives you something greater than education; it gives you revelation. Yes, in all your getting, get education (Proverbs 4:7); but also get revelation. God says that when you pray, it's an opportunity for Him to show you things you otherwise would not have known. It's a chance for Him to elevate your thinking and the amount of information you receive. It's a chance for Him to give you data and information you can't get anywhere else and any other way. God is offering you and I an opportunity for Him to open up our minds:

Prayer opens up portals that we mere mortals cannot penetrate on our own.

Moses said the secret things belong to God, and that which is revealed belongs to us and our children. (Deuteronomy 29:29)

Solomon, the wisest man who ever lived, was entrusted with power and position and prayed that God would give him wisdom. God gave him wisdom beyond his peers and wisdom beyond his years, all because he prayed. God showed him great and mighty things, gave him the wisdom to govern and get great wealth, and endowed him with insight on a myriad of subjects. (1 Kings 3:4-14)

James shared that if any of you lack wisdom, let him ask of God who gives liberally and without reproach, and it will be given. (James 1:5)

God wants to do something special in your personal prayer time. It's in the prayer closet that ideas are birthed, and visions are given. It's in prayer that clarity and comprehension come. When you pray, God will provide you with insight and understanding. Put yourself in a posture of prayer so God can mold your mind, shape your views, and transfer His thoughts to your soul. We ought to be running to pray every day! God has something He's trying to show us, tell us, and expose us to. There's something for us to hear, see, learn, discover, and unearth, things that eyes haven't seen nor ears heard (1 Corinthians 2:9). I don't want to miss anything the Creator wants to communicate to me, *do you*??.

Access To Resources

The real interpretation of things great and mighty is things *inaccessible*. God reminds us that there are some things we cannot access, some things we cannot get, because of the human limitations that we have. There are barriers, things that block us from attaining them. It may be education, training, a criminal past, a particular environment, or even physical limitations. But God says those things aren't a hindrance to Him. Prayer opens up those doors that we can't penetrate on our own. God says He will allow you to enter into certain places you didn't think you could get in and shouldn't get in, based on your limitations. He'll open up doors where you were locked out because of your credit score, education, or lack of connections. When you pray, God will open stuff up and let you in and allow you access.

Please understand there are some things *only* God can open up for you. There are some places *only* God can take you. He opens doors no man can shut. God will give you access to money for college, access to things for which your credit score or your income don't qualify, access to positions for which your training was not adequate to position you, and access to valuable and necessary data that you would not gain otherwise.

God can crack the codes. He can tap into some things, bypass some systems, and break down some walls that seem unscalable. Look around your life. Can you see that there are some things you're enjoying all because God opened the door for you to have the job, the home, the education, or the car you have? God gave you access!

God impresses the message that we shouldn't see praying as an empty or boring exercise or a bothersome task that does not yield results. He's telling us that He has things to show you, places to take you, blessings to give you; but, you won't get it unless you pray and spend time with Him. He's waiting on your call.

When they were smaller, my children would sometimes try and sneak to get something out of the cabinet, on the top shelf that was out of their reach. Sometimes I'd listen or stand back and just watch them struggle. Sometimes I'd hear them struggling to get it, but I wouldn't step in to help. It wasn't that I wanted to see them struggle, but I wanted them to come and ask me for help. On occasion, I'd turn away or act like I wasn't looking, and they would come over and grab me and point up to what they wanted. Then, I'd go and reach up with ease to grab what they wanted. I was just waiting for them to call me and ask me to give them what they wanted. While they were wrestling with it, I was just waiting for them to stop and turn to their father, who had greater access, and ask me to get what they desired.

Your Heavenly Father has some blessings on the top shelf you can't seem to reach. There are things you can't seem to get to, things that you have been struggling to obtain. You've been trying to get it. God is saying that He can get that for you; in fact, it's His joy to bless His children. He's just waiting for you to ask. He's just waiting for you to call, to say, "Father, I need you."

Won't you call on God today?

Section 7:

Getting Alone
with God

Mark 1:35-39

35 Now in the morning, having risen a long while before daylight, He went out and departed to a solitary place; and there He prayed.

36 And Simon and those who were with Him searched for Him.

37 When they found Him, they said to Him, "Everyone is looking for You."

38 But He said to them, "Let us go into the next towns, that I may preach there also, because for this purpose I have come forth."

39 And He was preaching in their synagogues throughout all Galilee, and casting out demons.

I believe God has great things that He wants to show you and share with you. Great things that are specially designed for you. But, for you to experience and receive those things, you're going to have to learn how to get alone with Him.

The Bible gives us a peek into the private prayer life of Jesus. We don't just see His public ministry; we also get a glimpse into His personal time with the Father. It was His constant communion with God that gave Him the power to perform His public service.

In the same way, if we are to be effective at whatever we are called to do, we must learn to develop the discipline of getting alone with God.

Prayer is one of the primary disciplines that Jesus prescribed to His disciples. He said when you pray, pray this way. When you fast, fast this way. When you give, give this way. Jesus even gave them an outline to use in prayer, providing a guide for what to ask and how to approach God (Matthew 6:1-18).

Most importantly, Jesus didn't just explain it to His disciples; He exemplified it before them. The Bible records in Luke 5:16 that He would often withdraw to the wilderness and pray. In other words, it was a habit — a discipline — that Jesus developed and demonstrated to His disciples.

Jesus had tough and difficult days. He had to deal with demons. He had to perform various public duties. From funerals to weddings, to visits to the sick and shut-in; from speaking engagements to witnessing and evangelizing; from confronting critical clergymen to developing doubting disciples—He had to stay prayed up. The Gospel of Mark is the shortest of the gospels. Mark opens and, in the first several verses, features Jesus at His baptism and beginning His public ministry. Mark doesn't deal with Jesus' birth or genealogies like Matthew and Luke. He starts off moving right into the life and servanthood of our Savior.

After starting His ministry, Jesus almost immediately called the first disciples, dealt with a demon-possessed person, healed Peter's mother, spoke at the temple, and responded to leaders who were opposing His work. All of this is enough to wear Him down and wear Him out. How did Jesus successfully navigate all of these things without burnout? It appears that Mark gives us the answer: The secret to His success was His supplication.

Jesus was very disciplined, and because of the discipline, He developed that same discipline in His disciples. I would like to use this section to discipline us to pray.

Chapter 1 of Mark provides us with some very practical principles we can adopt to develop a powerful prayer life. The Bible shares with us when Jesus prayed, where Jesus prayed, and why Jesus prayed.

CHAPTER 19

Prayer...Done on Schedule

Jesus Got Up Early Before His Day Began

Scripture says that long before the sun rose, the Son rose. Jesus got up early to get with His Heavenly Father and pray. The morning is the best time to meet with God. There is something serene, something special about that time just before sunrise. It invites us into a special time in the Spirit. The biblical record gives us several illustrations of the importance of early morning communion with God:

"With my soul I have desired You in the night, Yes by my spirit within me I will seek you early." (Isaiah 26:9)

"So it was, when the days of feasting had run their course, that Job would send and sanctify them, and he would rise early in the morning and offer burnt offering according to the number of them all." (Job 1:5)

"O God, You are my God; Early will I seek You; My soul thirsts for You; My flesh longs for You in a dry and thirsty land where there is no water." (Psalm 63:1)

As Isaiah, Job, David, and Jesus Himself bear witness, there is just something special about getting with God before sunrise. In his article "How to Maximize Your Morning," best-selling author Andy Andrews writes the following about the famous inventor George Washington Carver:

> *"You probably know him as the man who discovered 266 different uses for the peanut that we still use today.*
>
> *He was born a slave, but became one of the most impactful botanists and inventors to ever live. His accomplishments are simply astounding – how did he fit it all in?*
>
> *The simple answer is that he started every day while everyone else was still fast asleep. And while that's true – the master inventor* did *get up at 4 a.m. every morning – it's what he* did *after rising early that I believe made the biggest difference.*
>
> *After rising at 4 a.m., well before anyone else was awake, George Washington Carver would slip outside where it was very quiet and ask his Creator what he should get accomplished that day. Doing this, he explained, gave him his marching orders and let him go through his morning with a purpose that set the tone for the rest of the day.*
>
> *He believed strongly that this was the reason for his amazing productivity." (1)*

Carver was on the front line in the creation of new markets for farmers with the discovery of up to three hundred uses of peanuts, sweet potatoes, pecans, and soybeans. His list of discoveries surpasses even Ben Franklin's. God opened up his mind and imparted things to him. He gave him ideas and understanding and inventions and discoveries while he spent time with God early in the morning. I believe there are some things God wants to show you and share with you, but you have to be willing to get alone with God and spend some time with Him, so you can hear just what He wants you to know.

God wants to unlock some mysteries in your life. He wants to impart knowledge and understanding to you and maximize your mind's potential. He wants to tap into some of your hidden talents and help you hone gifts you didn't even know you had. Get alone with God, and He will show you some great things.

My kids know that when they come out with me by themselves, nine-times-out-of-ten, they're going to get a treat of some sort. In fact, they like to come back home and tell the others what we had to eat, or where we went, or show off their gift. They like to say, "Look what I got!" and, to the disappointed faces of the two that stayed behind, I say, "You should've come." See, some of the good things God has for you will only be received by you spending time alone with God one on one. Scripture says that if you, being evil, know how to give good gifts to your children, how much more will your Father who is in heaven give good things to those who ask Him? (Matthew 7:11) You'd best learn to get alone with God because He has something truly amazing in store for you.

There are some things God wants to say to you personally. Some things He wants to tell you away from everybody else. Most of the time, you'll discover that the people who received great revelations received them when they were alone within His presence.

While he was alone with God, Noah received a revelation to build the ark. (Genesis 6)

While he was alone with God, Abraham received the call to leave his home to walk into God's promised land. (Genesis 12)

While he was alone with God, Moses encountered God in a burning bush and later received the commandments on Mt. Sinai. (Exodus 3:19)

Samuel, Jeremiah, David, and Elijah all spent time on their own with God.

In fact, many of the most powerful people God used were loners. They didn't have a lot of running mates. They were by themselves, but they weren't alone. You may be by yourself, but you are not alone. Learn to get alone with God and see if He won't bring you satisfaction, contentment, joy, fulfillment, and even companionship. God will be everything that you need and will give you more than you can imagine.

We Need To Develop A Disciplined Prayer Life

Please don't get up for work or start your day and fail to pray. You don't want to do this or that, run here or there, before you have taken time to talk with God. Some of us jump into all kinds of tasks, errands, etc., and don't set aside time to pray. We just push it back and put it off, intending to get to it later. That "plan" usually results in no time given to God at all, or when we do, we're worn out and fall asleep in the middle of praying.

Give God the best of your time and the best of your mind. Offer to Him the first fruits of your day when your mind is fresh and receptive to His word. Don't pray *sporadically*; pray according to *schedule*. In other words, establish a predetermined time that you meet with the Lord and earnestly talk with Him. As we've discussed, it's best to set aside some time early in the morning to meet with God. But, even if it isn't early, make sure you have a specific, planned time for private fellowship with the Lord.

Daniel had a set time: morning, noon, and evening. He had disciplined himself to get with God. (Daniel 6:10)

The Jews had a set time, which the early church continued: morning, noon, and evening. (Psalm 55:17, Acts 3:1)

We need to develop these types of disciplines and have a set time we meet with God.

I once worked with a Muslim, and he would faithfully get his rug out and say his prayers. No matter what was happening, he would stop and pray. I noticed his discipline, and I was in awe. Even though I don't believe in his faith, I respected his discipline to pray that way. If he does that, surely those of us disciples connected to the true God should discipline ourselves to pray.

You and I need a disciplined life and prayer life like Jesus had. We should have an assigned time to get with God for prayer and meditation, perhaps followed by exercise and breakfast before starting our workday. I believe this may have been Jesus' schedule. He got up, went to the mountain (a secluded place or a secret place (Matthew 14:23), hiked for a time, and found a place to pray. Afterward, He would have enjoyed a walk-through nature, then jogged back to the disciples after eating a fig and barley granola bar and went to work. Can't you see it?!

As busy as Jesus was, He made space in His schedule to pray. I know we all work long, hard hours, and it's hard to find time to pray. I know it's not always easy, but we must understand prayer is a vital link between ourselves and God.

Prayer equips us to meet life's challenges.

Martin Luther said, "I have so much to do I can spend no less than the first 3 hours in prayer." (7)

Practice spending time in God's presence. Discipline yourself to be still. Jesus spent hours in prayer. He once asked His disciples if they really struggled to spend even one hour with Him in prayer (Matthew 26:40). Discipline yourself to learn how to spend one hour each day in prayer. Sit down, kneel, walk and talk, change positions, and go to different areas. Walk in the rooms or areas you want God to touch; the change of scenery will help to stimulate your prayer time. Spend that time alone with God. Sometimes you do have to be still and stay in the same spot — if the Spirit is telling you to be still, then be still. Be still and know that He is God (Psalm 46:10).

Praying is not a waste of time; it will actually *save* you time, and God will redeem that time you spend praying in preparation for your day. You have to learn to fight sleep and fatigue, and the devil will tell you that you're wasting time with a pointless, repetitious exercise. Make time to pray.

A company's young president instructed his secretary not to disturb him because he had an important meeting at a certain time each day. The chairman of the board came in one day and said that he wanted to see Mr. Jones immediately. His secretary apologized and told him that Mr. Jones could not be disturbed because he was in an important meeting. The chairman banged on the door and burst in and saw the president of the company on his knees in prayer. The chairman stepped out and asked the secretary if that was his usual practice. She confirmed that he did that every morning. The chairman responded, "No wonder I come to him for advice."

Meeting with God is your most important meeting in the morning. You and I can't afford to miss our time with God.

CHAPTER 20

Prayer...Done in Solitude

It Was A Chance To Retreat

Scripture says that Jesus often got alone with God. Finding solitude was important to Jesus; remember He often could not get away from crowds. Imagine people coming from miles around to hear Him, to get a touch from Him, to receive His counsel, to bring their loved ones who were sick and couldn't afford a doctor. Jesus often withdrew and was temporarily unavailable.

People wanted Jesus to perform weddings and funerals. They wanted Him to attend their parties and functions, to treat their children or heal their servants. In one passage, they tried to make him their king (John 6:15). So, scripture says that Jesus often withdrew Himself (Luke 5:16). He would go to the wilderness (Luke 4:1), or the mountains (Matthew 15:29; Luke 9:28), or perhaps a garden (Matthew 26:36). He retreated to the outdoors, where it was calm and peaceful. He walked or communed with God on these nature walks. There's something about being outdoors that has a way of making you feel closer to God.

Jesus would find a place to escape. Can you imagine hearing His prayers? What did He ask God or share with Him? What did they discuss during those private moments? Can you imagine being a proverbial "fly on the wall" to eavesdrop on the conversations? What did those days of prayer sound like? It's there in prayer where He could be free to express Himself and His deepest thoughts to God and receive what He needed to continue in ministry.

You and I need time alone with God so He can minister to us.

We don't just need any place; we need some seclusion. We need a place of solitude. We need a place where we get away from the hustle and bustle of life, a hiding place away from distractions like noise, pollution, other priorities, and even people, where God can transfer His thoughts to us and clear up the clutter and chaos in our minds and our lives. We need solitude so we can fully concentrate on Him.

Our lives are constantly filled with so much noise. It can be challenging to escape and slow down to meditate in peace and quiet. Some of us always have something on the TV, radio, or computer/internet—music, talk shows, functions, podcasts, social media, etc. We end up drained without even working hard. To really hear from God, we need a secret place where we can retreat and pray. Jesus said that when you pray, go to your secret place, shut the door, and your Father who sees in secret will reward you openly (Matthew 6:6).

The reason Jesus' public ministry is so powerful is because He has a powerful private ministry. Remember, our lives are lived from the inside out. The better your private life, the better your public life will be. What you give attention to in private is what will make the difference in public. If you are healthy inwardly, you will be more effective outwardly.

Your peace, joy, mental ability, faith, and ability to function properly, perform properly, and stay confident in the face of the devil and his imps will come through having spent time with God.

It Was A Chance To Be Renewed

Jesus was teaching that we need to take time out and talk to God. We need to let God revive us, restore our souls, restore our cells, and restore our very life. Every day we need to take time out in private to sit before the Lord so He can renew us.

Some of us are suffering from sensory overload. We find ourselves drained, tired, irritable, and possibly dealing with chronic fatigue as well as physical, emotional, mental, and spiritual exhaustion. We often experience all of this because we aren't taking time out to be renewed.

Every day I routinely put my cell phone on the charger so it can function properly. I take an hour every day and make sure it's plugged in. I don't want to go out having only 20 or 30 percent of life remaining; I need a full 100 percent to operate most effectively. Just like with our cellular devices, you need to plug in and pray. After a long day where people have pushed your buttons and life has left you drained, you need a recharge to be ready to go out and do it all again.

Jesus had to get with God because He gave so much of Himself to others. People who give out a lot to others need more moments to recharge. Parents, public servants, individuals who help or serve others — you need time with God to renew and recover and rejuvenate. Empathizing with others can empty you, and God provides us with the necessary refueling.

Some of us are the strongest ones in our circle, and people rely on us to function. We give out a lot of encouragement, advice, counsel, and help to others, so we really need God to revive and replenish us day by day. We need Him to pour into us because of all we are constantly pouring out.

Wherever I go, I make sure I have somewhere I can plugin. That's how prayer should be. Jesus said men ought always to pray and not faint (Luke 18:1). Prayer will keep you from running out of power, it will preserve you, and it will keep you from fainting. You could've and should've fallen out, but it's prayer that's helped you to keep functioning. While the research is limited, scientists have indicated that people who pray live longer lives and experience less anxiety and fear than people who do not pray or connect to God. Prayer works.

Jesus had to work and do ministry in tough environments and under stressful conditions, including dealing with demonically possessed people. He constantly saw and heard bad news and had people pulling and tugging Him to go here and there. He had to deal with hateful religious folks, lepers, and those facing other types of sickness, diseases, and death. He did all of this without falling apart because He trained Himself to get alone with God regularly. How about you?

CHAPTER 21

Prayer...Done to Gain Strength

Jesus' Prayer Produced Power

Please realize that you will sometimes be by yourself in prayer, and you won't always have others to pray with you and for you. It's good that you learn how to get with God for yourself, to encourage yourself in the Lord, and draw strength from Him.

The people we see who lived powerful lives had powerful prayer lives. Elijah had a powerful prayer life. David had a powerful prayer life. Paul had a powerful prayer life. Daniel had a powerful prayer life. Nehemiah had a powerful prayer life. If you are going to operate in the power of God and not be worn down, easily discouraged, dismayed, depressed, or distressed, you have to develop a powerful prayer life deliberately. Prayer equals power!!

Jesus prayed for the same reason we do. He was tempted in all points as we are. He had fear, frustration, and internal emotional battles. He had human weaknesses and limitations and depended on God as His source, just like us.

In Matthew 26, we find Jesus praying in the Garden of Gethsemane, a place where grapes were crushed. Instead, that night, it was Jesus who was coping in the crushing place. He was praying, and scripture says there was blood, sweat, and tears in that place. Jesus emptied himself in prayer. He was looking for support from His disciples at that moment but could find no one to pray with Him. Jesus lamented that His soul was deeply distressed, even unto the point of death. It's there He prays for strength and asks His Father if it's possible to let this cup pass from Him, crying out whether there was another way for Him to save the world than having to be brutally beaten and publicly humiliated. It's there that His humanity is most notable when He speaks His desire to avoid pain and suffering, but scripture says that the Father did not remove it, but instead gave Him the strength to go through it *after* he prayed. See, there are some things you're going to go through that will require you to learn how to get alone with God and spend time in prayer to have the power to face what you have to face. It may be a surgery. It may be a legal battle. It may be a difficult day. It may be a review at work. It may be having to arrange the funeral services of a loved one. But if you get with God, I promise you He will give you the power you need to deal with the problem you face.

DC Comic's Superman is one of the best-known superheroes across the world. In one of his stories, his father told him not to give up his power to be in a relationship with a human being, as there is no turning back after that change. Well, he lost his power. He was mistreated, beaten down, and overtaken by the enemy. Ultimately, he had to come back to his father to regain his strength in order to save the world. He returned to this secret place, beaten, wounded, hurt and confused, but he came out with power. Sometimes when you've been beaten down and wounded in life, you have to go before God in prayer. Tell the Father how much you need Him to save your world. Ask Him to help you. He can, and He will answer your prayer.

Something happens when you get alone with God. God has a way of giving you power and giving you strength. When you think you can't go further — pray. When you get tired and weary — pray. When the hurt doesn't seem to go away — pray. Get alone with God for a while. Pray!

"Have you not known? Have you not heard? The everlasting God, the Lord, The Creator of the ends of the earth, Neither faints nor is weary. His understanding is unsearchable. He gives power to the weak, and to those of us who have no might He increases strength." (Isaiah 20:28-29)

Prayer equals power. In those times when you need strength, go to your private place, and cry out to your Father. He will transfer His power and strength to you. When I'm weak...*He makes me strong.*

CONCLUSION

I will never forget the day we found out that my daughter Kennedy needed emergency surgery. She had been diagnosed with sickle cell anemia, a hereditary condition that causes red blood cells to change shape from being smooth, round, and flexible to the shape of a crescent (or sickle) and become stiff and sticky such that they can block blood flow and break down inside the blood vessels. Roxie and I were back and forth to the hospital when she was an infant, as she dealt with so many issues due to this condition. But on one occasion, when she was only 18 months old, the visit to Children's Hospital was not like the others. The doctors told us that her red blood cells had started to pool in her spleen, causing her blood to stop circulating through her body. They told us that without this surgery to remove her spleen, our baby could die.

I remember Roxie and I firing questions at the doctor about our options and alternatives to major surgery for our youngest daughter. They answered our questions, agreeing that the surgery was serious and that there were risks, but they could almost guarantee that she would not survive without it. As time was winding down, we finally consented to the procedure and found out that we could not be with her or even observe while they did it. I watched them wheel my baby girl down that hallway, not knowing what the outcome would be. I had so many emotions running through me I couldn't sit still. I remember feeling angry, scared, resentful, worried, and powerless. Here I was, a pastor who had comforted so many in this same hospital. Still, nothing anyone could say made me feel better as these mental images of my little girl with surgeons and scalpels and anesthesia and bright lights kept tumbling around in my mind. There are so many risks with surgery. I kept wondering if she would be okay--she was so young to be going through this major procedure. But, beyond that, I couldn't help but wonder what if the surgery was successful? What then? What would be her quality of life without a spleen? Would she be constantly ill? Would these visits to the hospital, these treatments, these doctors become the new normal for our family as she was susceptible to any number of illnesses? The worst part was there was nothing I could do but wait. I had always been a strong person, a natural leader.

When I wanted something, I went out and got it. I was a successful business owner, pastor of a rapidly growing church, an emerging influencer in the Indianapolis community. But here I was facing something that none of my skills or talents or achievements could address, and it was the most profound and most painful threat I had ever encountered. At that moment, I remember just pouring out my heart before God. I told Him everything I was feeling and everything I needed from Him on behalf of my family. I don't know how long I prayed in that hospital. I don't even know if anyone came in there while I was just emptying myself before God. But I remember, at one point, God stopped me in mid-sentence. He actually interrupted my lamentation and asked me who He was. I said, "I know You're God." Then He repeated the question, "Who am I?" and I answered again, "You're God." When He asked me a third time after that, I thought about how Jesus had questioned Peter by the Sea of Tiberias (John 21), and I knew God was trying to get me to understand something.

I started recalling everything He had been in my life. I started naming Him my Protector from the days of my youth when I ran the streets recklessly. I started naming Him my Savior from the day He came to me in a drug rehab center at the age of 19 and changed my entire life. I started naming Him my Guide as I had navigated through Bible college and church leadership. I started naming Him my Source, as He had gifted me with my amazing wife and my wonderful children. I started naming Him my Provider as I had walked away from barbering to pastoring full-time when the church wasn't even giving me a salary, and I had a young family to support. I started naming Him my Counselor, as I had to learn how to comfort those in distress.

God interrupted me again and told me that if He had been all of those things to me over the years, He had me now. He told me that He had my little girl in His hands and that I had nothing to worry about for her future. I wish I had the words to describe this release that came over me, as my fear and anxiety, and anger just miraculously fell away. I couldn't even understand it myself because in one minute, I was crying and repeating these words of frustration over and over again. Then I started answering God's questions, and my tears stopped flowing, my fists unclenched, and my whole face relaxed. I just felt lighter and peaceful. After some dialogue with God, my entire posture changed.

The next thing I knew, the surgeon came to us to report that the surgery had gone well, and Kennedy was going to be fine, just as God had said. In one of my most difficult moments, I sought God, and He answered me. Just like He said He would.

What God did through prayer for Hannah, Hezekiah, Elijah, Jeremiah, Christians in the first century, and Jesus Himself, He can and will do for us today. No matter the problem, God has a solution; you'll find it through prayer. No matter the question, God has an answer; you'll find it through prayer. No matter the confusion, God has the clarification; you'll find it through prayer. No matter the storm, God has both the umbrella and the sunshine; you'll find them through prayer. No matter the fear, God has a faith statement; you'll find it through prayer. No matter your downfall, God has a come up; you'll find it through prayer. Dear brother, dear sister, plug back into God with intentional prayer for your life. When you open the door, He will come in and blow your mind. I'm a witness several times over. You will be, too.

REFERENCES

(1) Andrews, Andy. "How to Maximize Your Morning." 29 September 2016. https://www.andyandrews.com/how-to-maximize-your-morning/

(2) Botelho, Jessica. "Prayer: An Act That Transforms." 02 October 2014. https://www.religiaodedeus.org/en/religion-part-our-daily-routine/prayer-act-transforms

(3) "Genesis 1:14-49 Day 4 The Sun's Shadow Moved Back." Institute of Biblical and Scientific Studies. https://www.bibleandscience.com/bible/books/genesis/genesis1_sunshadow.htm

(4) "George Muller: Trusting God for Daily Bread." Harvest Ministry. September 2020. http://harvestministry.org/muller

(5) "In U.S., Decline of Christianity Continues at Rapid Pace" www.pewforum.org. 17 October 2019.

(6) Karen Clark Sheard Testimony & The Glory Medley, YouTube, uploaded by UnitedToDance. 09 January 2016. https://www.youtube.com/watch?v=GSCYRmDR9cw

(7) Luther, Martin, Cyclopedia of Religious Anecdotes.
https://quotecatalog.com/quote/martin-luther-i-have-so-much-
MpxPPyp/#:~:text=%E2%80%9CI%20have%20so%20much%20to,to%20get%20it%20all%20done.%E2%80%9D&text=early%20until%20late.-
,In%20fact%2C%20I%20have%20so%20much%20to%20do%20that%20I,plans%20for%20the%20day%20were.

(8) Muller, George. "George Muller Persistent Prayer for 5 Individuals." 03 Jul 2017. https://www.georgemuller.org/devotional/george-muller-persistent-prayer-for-5-individuals.

(9) Rogers, Adrian. "The Privilege of Prayer." 18 May 2008. https://www.christianity.com/christian-life/prayer/the-privilege-of-prayer-11549313.html.

(10) Rogers, Kristen. "The Psychological Benefits of Prayer." 17 June 2020. https://www.cnn.com/2020/06/17/health/benefits-of-prayer-wellness/index.html.

(11) Spurgeon, Charles. "Praying in the Spirit: Fervency." 15 Oct 2007. http://paul.dubuc.org/2007/10/15/charles-spurgeon-praying-in-the-holy-spirit-fervency/